my World

Social Studies®

Making Our Way

PEARSON

Boston, Massachusetts
Chandler, Arizona
Glenview, Illinois
New York, New York

It's my story, too!

You are one of the authors of this book. You can write in this book! You can take notes in this book! You can draw in it, too! This book will be yours to keep.

Print your name, school, and city or town below. Then write to tell everyone all about you.

Name

School

City or Town

All About Me

Credits appear on pages **R24–R25,** which constitute an extension of this copyright page.

Softcover: ISBN-13: 978-0-328-81350-6
               ISBN-10: 0-328-81350-8
               13 18

Hardcover: ISBN-13: 978-0-328-84904-8
               ISBN-10: 0-328-84904-9
               4 15

PEARSON

Built for Texas

Pearson *Texas myWorld Social Studies* was developed especially for Texas with the help of teachers from across the state and covers 100 percent of the Texas Essential Knowledge and Skills for Social Studies. This story began with a series of teacher roundtables in cities across the state of Texas that inspired a program blueprint for *Texas myWorld Social Studies*. In addition, Judy Brodigan served as our expert advisor, guiding our creation of a dynamic Social Studies curriculum for TEKS mastery. Once this blueprint was finalized, a dedicated team—made up of Pearson authors, content experts, and social studies teachers from Texas—worked to bring our collective vision into reality.

Pearson would like to extend a special thank you to all of the teachers who helped guide the development of this program. We gratefully acknowledge your efforts to realize the possibilities of elementary Social Studies teaching and learning. Together, we will prepare Texas students for their future roles in college, careers, and as active citizens.

Program Consulting Authors

The Colonial Williamsburg Foundation
Williamsburg VA

Armando Cantú Alonzo
Associate Professor of History
Texas A&M University
College Station TX

Dr. Linda Bennett
Associate Professor, Department of
Learning, Teaching, & Curriculum
College of Education
University of Missouri
Columbia MO

Dr. James B. Kracht
Byrne Chair for Student Success
Executive Associate Dean
College of Education and Human
Development
College of Education
Texas A&M University
College Station TX

Dr. William E. White
Vice President for Productions,
Publications and Learning
Ventures
The Colonial Williamsburg
Foundation
Williamsburg VA

Reviewers and Consultants

ACADEMIC REVIEWERS

Kathy Glass
Author, *Lesson Design for Differentiated Instruction*
President, Glass Educational
Consulting
Woodside CA

Roberta Logan
African Studies Specialist
Retired, Boston Public Schools/
Mission Hill School
Boston MA

Jeanette Menendez
Reading Coach
Doral Academy Elementary
Miami FL

Bob Sandman
Adjunct Assistant Professor of
Business and Economics
Wilmington College—Cincinnati
Branches
Blue Ash OH

PROGRAM CONSULTANT

Judy Brodigan
Former President, Texas Council
for Social Studies
Grapevine TX

Padre Island National Seashore

CONNECT

Master the TEKS with a personal connection.

myStory Spark

The **myStory Book** writing strand in the program begins with a **myStory Spark** activity. Here you can record your initial ideas about the **Big Question**.

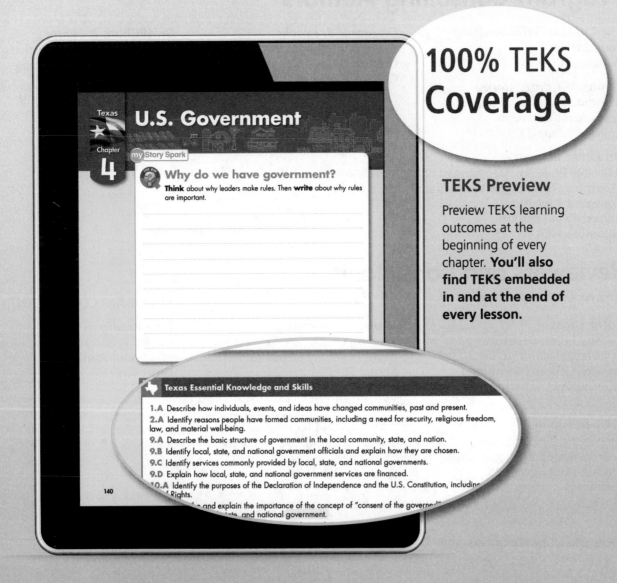

Texas

Chapter 4

U.S. Government

my Story Spark

Why do we have government?
Think about why leaders make rules. Then **write** about why rules are important.

Texas Essential Knowledge and Skills

1.A Describe how individuals, events, and ideas have changed communities, past and present.
2.A Identify reasons people have formed communities, including a need for security, religious freedom, law, and material well-being.
9.A Describe the basic structure of government in the local community, state, and nation.
9.B Identify local, state, and national government officials and explain how they are chosen.
9.C Identify services commonly provided by local, state, and national governments.
9.D Explain how local, state, and national government services are financed.
10.A Identify the purposes of the Declaration of Independence and the U.S. Constitution, including Rights.
and explain the importance of the concept of "consent of the governed" and national government.

140

100% TEKS Coverage

TEKS Preview

Preview TEKS learning outcomes at the beginning of every chapter. **You'll also find TEKS embedded in and at the end of every lesson.**

Lesson list

- **Lesson 1** America's First Peoples
- **Lesson 2** Early Explorers
- **Lesson 3** Early Spanish Communities
- **Lesson 4** Early French Communities
- **Lesson 5** Early English Communities
- **Lesson 6** Creating a New Nation

Mission San Luis
A Multicultural Community

myStory Video

From about 1560 to 1690, there were more than 100 Spanish missions built throughout Florida. A mission is a settlement that has a church where religion is taught. One of the most famous missions is Mission San Luis. Located in Tallahassee, it is one of the last remaining mission sites today. "It's also the only place where both the Apalachee and the Spaniards lived together," says Grace. The Apalachee are Native Americans and Spaniards are people from Spain. "I love learning about other cultures," she adds. No one lives at the mission anymore, but it has been rebuilt. Visitors can tour the mission and watch people act out what life was like there hundreds of years ago.

"Native Americans and Spaniards shared this mission," Grace explains. At that time, Native Americans and European settlers usually did not live together. Mission San Luis was special.

Grace was excited to visit one of the last remaining missions.

Mission San Luis

myStory Video

Move seamlessly from **the Student Worktext** to technology! Watch the myStory Videos to explore the **Big Question** and key ideas in the chapter.

Access the TEKS

Texas *myWorld Social Studies* covers the TEKS in all formats. Access the content through the printed worktext, eText, or online with the digital course on Realize.

 PEARSON **realize** **Go online at:** www.PearsonTexas.com

Every lesson is supported by digital activities, myStory Videos, vocabulary activities, and myStory Book on Tikatok.

Enjoy social studies while practicing the TEKS.

Student Interactive Worktext

With the Texas *myWorld Social Studies* worktext, you'll love writing, drawing, circling and underlining in your own book.

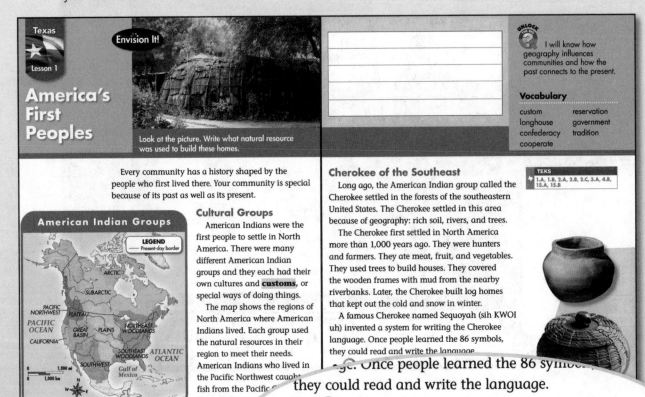

Texas — Lesson 1

Envision It!

America's First Peoples

Look at the picture. Write what natural resource was used to build these homes.

UNLOCK I will know how geography influences communities and how the past connects to the present.

Vocabulary

custom	reservation
longhouse	government
confederacy	tradition
cooperate	

Every community has a history shaped by the people who first lived there. Your community is special because of its past as well as its present.

American Indian Groups

LEGEND — Present-day border

ARCTIC, SUBARCTIC, PACIFIC NORTHWEST, PLATEAU, PACIFIC OCEAN, GREAT BASIN, PLAINS, CALIFORNIA, NORTHEAST WOODLANDS, SOUTHEAST WOODLANDS, ATLANTIC OCEAN, SOUTHWEST, Gulf of Mexico

Cultural Groups

American Indians were the first people to settle in North America. There were many different American Indian groups and they each had their own cultures and **customs**, or special ways of doing things.

The map shows the regions of North America where American Indians lived. Each group used the natural resources in their region to meet their needs. American Indians who lived in the Pacific Northwest caught fish from the Pacific C... Those living on... the rich soil th...

1. Identify and underline two ways A... used natural resources to live.

Cherokee of the Southeast

Long ago, the American Indian group called the Cherokee settled in the forests of the southeastern United States. The Cherokee settled in this area because of geography: rich soil, rivers, and trees.

The Cherokee first settled in North America more than 1,000 years ago. They were hunters and farmers. They ate meat, fruit, and vegetables. They used trees to build houses. They covered the wooden frames with mud from the nearby riverbanks. Later, the Cherokee built log homes that kept out the cold and snow in winter.

A famous Cherokee named Sequoyah (sih KWOI uh) invented a system for writing the Cherokee language. Once people learned the 86 symbols, they could read and write the language.

TEKS 1.A, 1.B, 2.A, 2.B, 2.C, 3.A, 4.B, 15.A, 15.B

...ge. Once people learned the 86 sym... they could read and write the language.

2.  **Main Idea and Details Describe** how the Cherokee created a new community.

Target Reading Skills

The worktext enables you to practice important **Target Reading Skills**—essential skills you'll need when reading informational texts. Reinforce your ELA TEKS during the social studies block of time.

PEARSON realize Go online at: www.PearsonTexas.com

Every lesson is supported by digital activities, myStory Videos, vocabulary activities, and myStory Book on Tikatok.

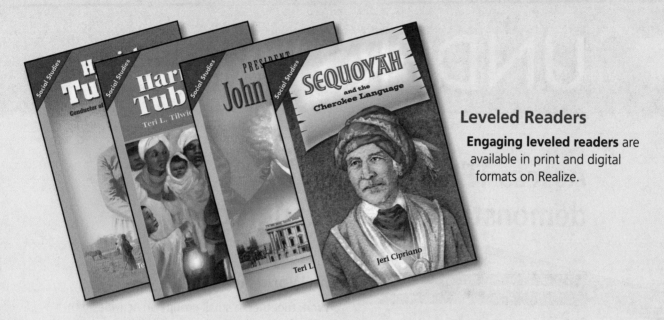

Leveled Readers

Engaging leveled readers are available in print and digital formats on Realize.

Digital Activities

Every lesson includes a **Digital Activity** that helps support the Big Idea.

UNDERSTAND

Assess TEKS and demonstrate understanding.

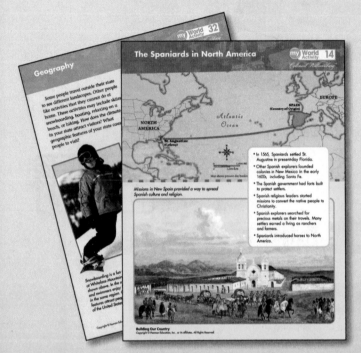

myWorld Activities

Work together in small groups on activities that range from mapping, graphing, and role playing, to read-alouds and analyzing primary sources. Digital versions of innovative hands-on activities for each chapter can be found on Realize.

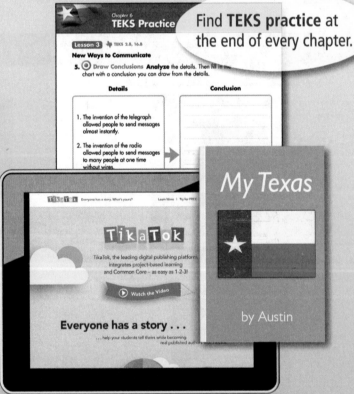

Find **TEKS practice** at the end of every chapter.

myStory Book

The **myStory Book** final writing activity gives you the exciting opportunity to write and illustrate your own digital book. Go to **www.Tikatok.com/myWorldSocialStudies** to learn more.

My School, My Community

PEARSON
realize. Go online at:
www.PearsonTexas.com

- ▶ Interactive eText
- ▶ Big Question Activity
  How do people best cooperate?
- ▶ myStory Video
  How do people best cooperate?
- ▶ Song
  Lyrics and Music
- ▶ Vocabulary Preview
- ▶ Lesson Introduction
- ▶ Digital Got it? Activity
- ▶ Digital Skill Lessons
  Problem Solving
  Fact and Opinion
- ▶ Vocabulary Review
- ▶ myStory Book on Tikatok
  www.tikatok.com/
  myWorldSocialStudies
- ▶ Chapter Tests

THE BIG ? How do people best cooperate?

Work in the Community

? **How do people get what they need?**

Texas

Chapter

3

Looking at Our World

Traditions We Share

How is culture shared?

PEARSON realize Go online at:
www.PearsonTexas.com

- ⊙ **Interactive eText**
- ⊙ **Big Question Activity**
  How is culture shared?
- ⊙ **myStory Video**
  How is culture shared?
- ⊙ **Song**
  Lyrics and Music
- ⊙ **Vocabulary Preview**
- ⊙ **Lesson Introduction**
- ⊙ **Digital Got it? Activity**
- ⊙ **Digital Skill Lessons**
  Compare and Contrast
  Using Graphic Sources
- ⊙ **Vocabulary Review**
- ⊙ **myStory Book on Tikatok**
  www.tikatok.com/
  myWorldSocialStudies
- ⊙ **Chapter Tests**

Our Past, Our Present

? **THE BIG** How does life change throughout history?

Keys to Good Writing

The Writing Process

Good writers follow steps when they write. Here are five steps that will help you become a good writer!

Prewrite	Plan your writing.
Draft	Write your first draft.
Revise	Make your writing better.
Edit	Check your writing.
Share	Share your writing with others.

21st Century Learning Online Tutor

21C

You can go online to www.PearsonTexas.com to practice the skills listed below.
These are skills that will be important to you throughout your life.
After you complete each skill tutorial online, check it off here in your worktext.

⊙ Target Reading Skills

☐ Main Idea and Details   ☐ Generalize

☐ Cause and Effect   ☐ Compare and Contrast

☐ Classify and Categorize   ☐ Sequence

☐ Fact and Opinion   ☐ Summarize

☐ Draw Conclusions

21C Collaboration and Creativity Skills

☐ Solve Problems   ☐ Resolve Conflict

☐ Work in Cooperative Teams   ☐ Generate New Ideas

21C Graph Skills

☐ Interpret Graphs   ☐ Interpret Timelines

☐ Create Charts

21C Map Skills

☐ Use Longitude and Latitude   ☐ Interpret Economic Data on Maps

☐ Interpret Physical Maps   ☐ Interpret Cultural Data on Maps

21C Critical Thinking Skills

☐ Compare Viewpoints   ☐ Make Decisions

☐ Use Primary and Secondary Sources   ☐ Predict Consequences

☐ Identify Bias

21C Media and Technology Skills

☐ Conduct Research   ☐ Evaluate Media Content

☐ Use the Internet Safely   ☐ Deliver an Effective Presentation

☐ Analyze Images

Celebrate Freedom

TEKS
13.A, 14.D, 18.B

Freedom to Choose

Freedom is a person's right to make choices. One choice we have in our country is to vote. A **vote** is a choice that gets counted. Each person gets one vote.

You can vote in class to make a group decision. You can vote to choose a game to play. Voting is a tradition that celebrates freedom!

1. **Underline** what we are free to do in our country.

Vocabulary

vote

mayor

1

Freedom to Vote

People have the freedom to make important decisions in our country. One decision is to vote for our leaders.

A mayor is a community leader. The **mayor** is the head of a town or city.

The mayor works with other leaders. They make sure we are safe. They make sure the community has everything it needs to run smoothly.

2. What is a decision people can make in our country?

_____

_____

_____

It's Time to Vote!

- **Make** a poster to get people to vote.

- **Draw** a colorful picture. Add details.

- **Write** a slogan or sentence.

- **Tell** why it is important to vote.

Look at all the posters in your class. Vote for
the three posters you like best.

The Alamo

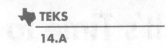

Long ago, Texas was part of Mexico. Texans wanted freedom.

Vocabulary

mission

The Alamo was a Spanish **mission,** or church, in San Antonio. Texans who wanted freedom captured the city in December, 1835. They used the Alamo as their camp.

Soon, many Mexican soldiers attacked the Alamo. The Texans fought back but lost the battle. The Alamo became a symbol of the fight for freedom.

1. Why is the Alamo an important symbol?

_____

_____

_____

Sam Houston

★ TEKS
2.A

Sam Houston and other Texans still wanted Texas to be free. On April 21, 1836, he and his army won the Battle of San Jacinto. Soldiers shouted "Remember the Alamo" during the battle. Texas won its **independence,** or freedom.

Each year, we celebrate freedom on San Jacinto Day.

Vocabulary

independence

1. **Underline** facts about how Sam Houston was an important leader.

2. **Circle** what people do on San Jacinto Day.

SAM HOUSTON
1793 1863

5

Welcome to Texas

A Map of Texas

Texas is one of the 50 states in the United States. The main cities are shown on the map. Austin is the capital of Texas. That is why it has a star.

You can use different maps to locate the United States, Texas, and your community. Some maps show small towns as well as big cities.

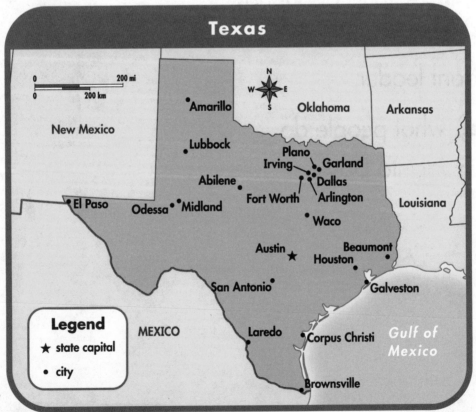

TEKS
5.B

Vocabulary

border

6

Four states **border,** or are next to, Texas.
They are New Mexico, Oklahoma, Arkansas,
and Louisiana. The country of Mexico borders
Texas, too. It is west of Texas. The Gulf of
Mexico is east of Texas.

You can locate your community on maps of
Texas, too. If your community is not named
on the map, start by finding nearby cities. Use
them to locate your community.

1. Circle the capital city on the map.

2. **Mark** an *X* on the map to show where
   you live.
   Write the name of the community
   where you live.

3. Use a globe to **locate** the
   United States and Texas.

Texas Motto
Friendship

A **motto** is a saying. It reminds people of what is important. The motto for Texas is "Friendship."

Long ago, Texas was called *Tejas* in Spanish. It comes from an American Indian word. It means "friends."

1. **Underline** the Texas motto.

2. **Draw** a picture of what the Texas motto means to you.

Vocabulary

motto

"Texas, Our Texas"

TEKS
14.C

An **anthem** is a song of praise. The anthem for our state is called "Texas, Our Texas." It reminds us of what is important about where we live.

Vocabulary

anthem

God bless you Texas!
And keep you brave and strong,
That you may grow in power
  and worth,
Throughout the ages long.

1. **Underline** words in the anthem that tell about Texas.

9

The United States Flag
Pledge of Allegiance

TEKS
14.B

One patriotic symbol for our country is a flag. We say a **pledge,** or promise, to it. We promise to be loyal. We promise to show we care about our country, too.

Vocabulary

pledge

I pledge allegiance to the Flag of the United States of America and to the Republic for which it stands, one Nation under God, indivisible, with liberty and justice for all.

1. **Circle** sentences that tell why we say the Pledge of Allegiance.

2. **Recite** the Pledge of Allegiance.

The Texas Flag
Our Pledge

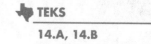
TEKS
14.A, 14.B

The Texas flag is a patriotic **symbol** that stands for our state. We say a pledge to it. We promise to show we care about our state. We promise to respect it, too.

Vocabulary

symbol

> Honor the Texas flag; I pledge allegiance to thee, Texas, one state under God, one and indivisible.

1. **Underline** a patriotic symbol that stands for Texas.

2. **Recite** the pledge to the Texas flag.

3. **Tell** why you say a pledge to it.

My School, My Community

 my Story Spark

THE BIG ? How do people best cooperate?

Draw a picture of yourself being a good citizen in school.

my Story Video

⭐ Texas Essential Knowledge and Skills

11.A Explain the purpose for rules and laws in the home, school, and community.

11.B Identify rules and laws that establish order, provide security, and manage conflict.

12.A Identify the responsibilities of authority figures in the home, school, and community.

12.B Identify and describe the roles of public officials in the community, state, and nation.

12.C Identify and describe the role of a good citizen in maintaining a constitutional republic.

13.A Identify characteristics of good citizenship, including truthfulness, justice, equality, respect for oneself and others, responsibility in daily life, and participation in government by educating oneself about the issues, respectfully holding public officials to their word, and voting.

13.B Identify historical figures such as Benjamin Franklin, Francis Scott Key, and Eleanor Roosevelt who have exemplified good citizenship.

14.A Explain state and national patriotic symbols, including the United States and Texas flags, the Liberty Bell, the Statue of Liberty, and the Alamo.

14.B Recite and explain the meaning of the Pledge of Allegiance to the United States Flag and the Pledge to the Texas Flag.

14.C Identify anthems and mottoes of Texas and the United States.

14.D Explain and practice voting as a way of making choices and decisions.

14.E Explain how patriotic customs and celebrations reflect American individualism and freedom.

14.F Identify Constitution Day as a celebration of American freedom.

17.B Obtain information about a topic using a variety of valid visual sources such as pictures, symbols, electronic media, maps, literature, and artifacts.

17.C Sequence and categorize information.

18.A Express ideas orally based on knowledge and experiences.

18.B Create and interpret visual and written material.

19.A Use a problem-solving process to identify a problem, gather information, list and consider options, consider advantages and disadvantages, choose and implement a solution, and evaluate the effectiveness of the solution.

 Begin With a Song

You're a Grand Old Flag

by George M. Cohan

You're a grand old flag,
You're a high flying flag
And forever in peace may you wave.
You're the emblem of the land I love,
The home of the free and the brave.

Vocabulary Preview

- citizen
- responsibility
- right
- law
- vote

GROCERY STORE

STOP

VOTE HERE

George Washington

President of the United States of America

Vote For GARZA For Governor

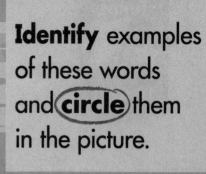

Identify examples of these words and ⬭circle⬭ them in the picture.

Meet The Governor

1897

CITY HALL

55

STOP

NO PARKING ANY TIME

leader

government

governor

president

symbol

15

I Am a Good Citizen

Circle someone who is being helpful.

TEKS
11.A, 13.A, 14.B, 17.B, 18.A, 18.B

A **citizen** is a person who belongs to a state or country. Good citizens work to make things better. They help others. They follow rules. They tell the truth and are just, or fair. Good citizens respect themselves and others, too. These are responsibilities of good citizens. A **responsibility** is something you should do.

1. ◎ **Fact and Opinion**
   Underline facts above that tell how good citizens are responsible each day.

16

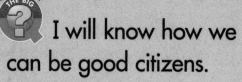
Vocabulary

citizen
responsibility
community

Citizens at School

You can be a good citizen at school. You can help others. You can follow rules. You can work well in groups.

Good citizens care about our country. We show this when we say the Pledge of Allegiance. The Pledge says we will be true to our country.

2. **Write** one way you can be a good citizen at school.

_____

_____

_____

Citizens in the Community

A **community** is the place where people live, work, and play. You can be a good citizen in your community. You can follow community rules. You can do things that help others. You can help keep the community clean.

3. **Underline** ways above that tell how to be a good citizen in your community.

Picking up roadside litter

4. ⊙ **Main Idea and Details** **Read** the sentences below. **Underline** the main idea.

I am a good citizen. I tell the truth. I am just, or fair. I follow the rules. I put trash where it should go.

5. 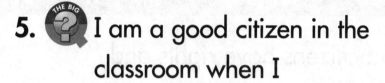 I am a good citizen in the classroom when I

6. **Draw** two pictures on a separate piece of paper. Show two ways you are a responsible citizen each day.

7. **Turn and talk** to a partner. **Identify** characteristics of good citizenship. **Tell** how you can show each characteristic.

PEARSON realize Go online to access your interactive digital lesson.

19

My Rights and Responsibilities

These children are helping at home.

TEKS
13.A, 17.B, 17.C, 18.A, 18.B

Good citizens have rights and responsibilities. A **right** is what you are free to do or have. A responsibility is a thing you should do.

1. **Look** at the picture. What responsibility does the girl have?

Draw one way you can help at home.

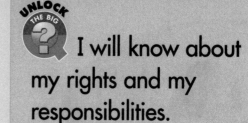
Vocabulary

right

cooperate

My Rights

You have rights at home and at school. You have the right to speak up. You have the right to belong to a group. You also have the right to laugh, talk, and play.

2. ◎ **Main Idea and Details** Circle the main idea above. **Underline** the detail sentences.

My Responsibilities

You have daily responsibilities at home. One may be to keep your room clean. Others may be to do your homework and to always tell the truth.

You have daily responsibilities at school. One is to do your best work. Others are to follow rules and take turns.

3. **Mark** the boxes that show your daily responsibilities.

My Daily Responsibilities

At Home	At School
☐ feed a pet	☐ take turns
☐ set the table	☐ get along with others
☐ clean my room	☐ follow rules
☐ tell the truth	☐ do my best work

It is your responsibility to cooperate with others. When you **cooperate,** you work together and show respect. You do not bully. You work well with others.

🔺 TEKS 13.A, 18.A, 18.B

4. ◎ **Fact and Opinion Read** the sentence below. **Write** whether it is a fact or an opinion.

You have the right to belong to a group.

_____

5. ❓ A classroom responsibility I have is to

_____

6. **Write** on another piece of paper. **List** ways you show respect for yourself and others. **Turn and talk** to a classmate about your experiences of showing respect.

Collaboration and Creativity

Problem Solving

A problem is something to be worked out.

A solution is an answer to a problem.

1. Identify the problem.

2. Gather information about it.

3. List ways to fix it.

4. Ask: "Which way will work best?"

5. Choose a way and fix the problem.

6. Think about how well your plan worked.

TEKS

SS 19.A Use a problem-solving process to identify a problem, gather information, list and consider options, consider advantages and disadvantages, choose and implement a solution, and evaluate the effectiveness of the solution.

Try it!

1. **Name** the problem. Use the steps on page 24 to fix the problem.

2. **Draw** a picture. Show one way the children can fix the problem. **Tell** why this plan works best.

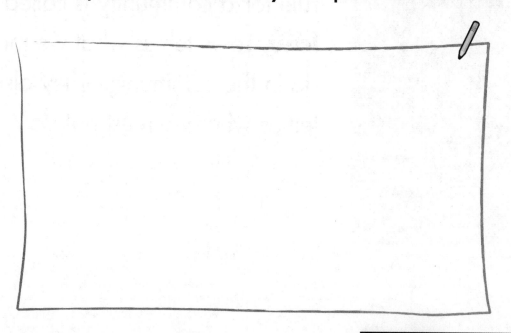

PEARSON realize Go online to access your interactive digital lesson.

25

I Follow Rules and Laws

(Circle) the signs that show what people should or should not do.

TEKS
11.A, 11.B, 17.B, 17.C, 18.A, 18.B

You brush your teeth after eating a meal. That is a home rule. You share books. That is a class rule. Rules tell us what to do. Rules also tell us what not to do.

Communities have rules, too. A rule for a community is called a **law.** Laws tell us what we must do in the community. They also tell us what we must not do.

NO Swimming

Main Street

First

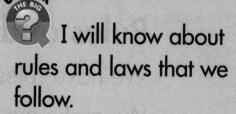

UNLOCK THE BIG ? I will know about rules and laws that we follow.

Vocabulary

law

Rules and Laws

Rules and laws establish order and keep things fair. We raise our hands to say something in class.

Some rules and laws provide security. These rules keep us safe. We wear seat belts in a car.

Other rules and laws manage conflict. They help us get along with others. We take turns and share.

1. ⊙ **Fact and Opinion**
   <u>Underline</u> three facts that tell why we have rules and laws.

PEARSON realize · · · · | Go online to access your interactive digital lesson.

27

Rules and Laws at Home

We have rules at home. We take care of our things. We make our beds. We clean our rooms.

Home rules keep things fair. We all do our part to help out. We take turns feeding pets. We take turns setting the table, too.

Rules and laws help us stay safe and healthy. We put our toys away so no one gets hurt. We wash our hands before eating. That rule keeps us healthy.

2. Underline rules and laws that establish order and keep things fair.

Rules and Laws at School

Rules and laws at school are important. They help us get along with one another. We are nice to people. We leave other people's things alone. We listen to friends when they talk. We say "Please" and "Thank you."

We share the computer. We take turns on the playground. We work together in class. We help each other clean up, too.

3. **Write** one rule that helps you manage conflict and get along with classmates.

Rules and Laws in the Community

Rules and laws in the community are important, too.

One law is that children must go to school. This law makes sure all children have an education. Another law is to put trash where it should go. This law keeps our community clean.

We have rules and laws that keep us safe, or provide security. We wear a helmet when we ride a bike. Cars must stop at STOP signs.

Rules and laws establish order, too. These rules and laws can be different in different places. Some communities have laws about walking dogs on a leash.

4. **Underline** rules and laws that keep us safe.

5. ⊙ **Compare and Contrast** What is one rule you follow both at home and at school?

6. ❓ One rule or law I follow in my community is

7. **Draw** two pictures on a separate piece of paper. Show yourself following a rule. Show what would happen if nobody followed that rule. **Write** the rule under the drawings.

8. **Turn and talk** to a partner. Name rules and laws at home, at school, and in the community. **Explain** the purpose for each one.

Texas

Lesson 4

My Leaders

Envision It!

Circle people who are in charge.

TEKS
12.A, 17.B, 17.C, 18.A, 18.B

A **leader** is an authority figure. A leader helps people decide what to do. Leaders can make rules. They make sure we follow rules, too.

Leaders help us at home, at school, and in the community. One leader at school is the principal.

1. **Fill in** the blank using the details above to help you.

The _____

makes rules for a school.

Vocabulary

leader

Leaders at Home

We have leaders at home. They can be mothers and fathers. They can be grandparents. Older brothers and sisters can be leaders, too.

Leaders at home keep you safe. They keep you healthy. They make rules so everyone gets along.

2. ◉ **Fact and Opinion Read** the sentences below. Circle the opinion.

A grandparent is a leader.

Grandparents are the best leaders.

PEARSON realize Go online to access your interactive digital lesson.

33

Leaders at School

The principal and teachers are leaders at school. They help you follow rules. Other school leaders keep you safe. They make sure you follow rules on the bus and at lunch. Coaches make sure you play fair.

You can be a leader, too. One way is to do a classroom job. Another way is to be a team captain.

Leaders in the Community

Many community leaders keep people safe. They make sure people follow laws. Police officers make sure people stop at red lights. Firefighters keep people safe from a fire. Doctors help sick people feel better.

3. Fill in the blank.

We have leaders at home, at school,

and in the _____ .

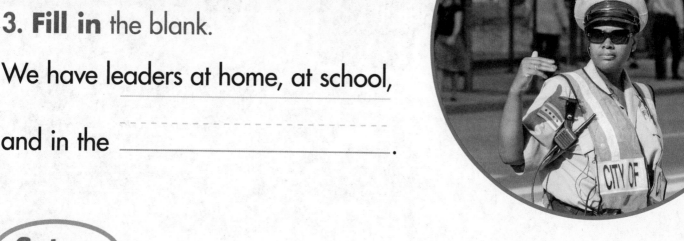

 **Got it?**

TEKS 12.A, 17.C, 18.A

4. ⊙ **Main Idea and Details** **Read** the sentences below. (Circle) the main idea.

A coach is a school leader. The coach teaches children how to play sports.

5. ❓ A leader in my school helps us by

 my Story Ideas

_____

6. Draw a chart on a separate piece of paper. **Write** Home, School, and Community at the top. **Explain** how leaders help us in each place.

7. Turn and talk to a partner. Take turns identifying authority figures and their responsibilities.

Texas

Lesson 5

My Government

Circle the people who work for the community.

TEKS
12.B, 12.C, 13.A, 14.D, 17.B, 18.B

Think what might happen if no one was in charge. There would be no one to help make our rules and laws.

A **government** is made up of citizens. They are in charge. They work together to make rules and laws. They work so all citizens get what they need.

We have three kinds of government. We have government for our community, our state, and our country.

Government leaders meet in a community.

36

Vocabulary

government   president

mayor   vote

governor

Community Government

The **mayor** is the leader in many communities. Other public officials work with the mayor in community government.

These leaders make rules and laws for the community. They make sure there are police and firefighters. They make sure trash is collected.

1. ◎ **Fact and Opinion** <u>Underline</u> facts above that describe the role of public officials in the community.

The Capitol in Austin, Texas

State Government

The leader of a state is the **governor.** The governor works with other leaders in the state government.

These leaders keep the state running smoothly. They make rules and laws for the state. They decide how the state spends money.

State leaders care for the people in the state. They make sure the state has schools. They make sure roads, bridges, and tunnels are safe. They give money for state parks, too.

2. **Write** a sentence. Tell about one role of state leaders.

_____

_____

_____

_____

National Government

Our country is a constitutional republic. It has a plan for government called the Constitution. Citizens choose leaders to act for them in the government. These leaders follow the plan.

President Barack Obama

The leader of our country is the **president.** The president and other public officials work for all of our country's citizens. They make laws for our country.

The national government makes sure all people are treated fairly and equally. It keeps citizens safe. It makes sure that mail gets to the right places.

3. **Fill in** the blank. Use the details above to help you.

Our country is a _____

_____

_____ .

Citizens and Government

Citizens are part of our government. We help to maintain, or keep up, the constitutional republic. We do this when we vote. To **vote** is to make a choice that is counted. Each person has one vote. Voting is a way for groups to make decisions.

Voting is a right for citizens in our country. Voting is also a way we show good citizenship.

Citizens vote to choose our leaders. Our leaders act for us. Citizens ask leaders to work hard. We ask them to keep their word, or promise, too.

Citizens sometimes vote to decide important questions. It is our responsibility to learn about the issues. Then we can make good decisions when we vote.

4. **Underline** what we ask leaders to do.

TEKS 12.B, 12.C, 13.A, 14.D, 18.B

5. 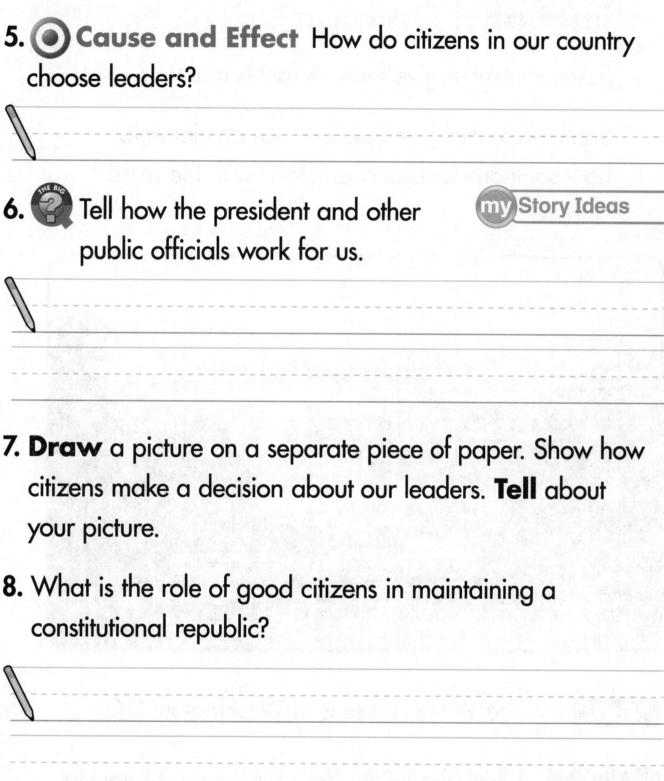**Cause and Effect** How do citizens in our country choose leaders?

6. Tell how the president and other public officials work for us.

my Story Ideas

7. **Draw** a picture on a separate piece of paper. Show how citizens make a decision about our leaders. **Tell** about your picture.

8. What is the role of good citizens in maintaining a constitutional republic?

Fact and Opinion

Some sentences give facts. A fact is true.

Some sentences give opinions. An opinion tells how someone feels. It often starts with the words "I think."

Fact   The White House is in Washington, D.C.

Opinion   I think the White House is the most beautiful building in Washington, D.C.

TEKS

SS 17.B Obtain information about a topic using a variety of valid visual sources.
ELA 4.B Locate facts and details about stories and other texts.

1. **Look** at the picture. **Read** the sentences below it.

I think firefighters have the most important job.

Firefighters work together to put out fires.

2. **Underline** the sentence that gives a fact.

3. **Circle** the sentence that gives an opinion.

PEARSON **realize** | Go online to access your interactive digital lesson.

43

Symbols of My Country

Circle the flag of our country.

TEKS
★ 13.B, 14.A, 14.B, 14.C, 14.E, 14.F, 17.B, 18.A, 18.B

Uncle Sam is a symbol of our country.

Our country is the United States of America. Our country has many national symbols. A **symbol** is something that stands for something else. Our red, white, and blue flag is a patriotic symbol of our country. There are 13 red and white stripes, one for each of the original colonies. There are 50 white stars, one for each state.

1. **Explain** the United States flag to a partner. Explain how it stands for our country.

44

American Symbols

The Statue of Liberty stands for hope and freedom. The Liberty Bell also stands for freedom. The White House stands for the government of our country. It is where the president lives and works. "In God We Trust" is a motto, or saying. It reminds us about what is important to our country.

2. Fill in the blank to explain national patriotic symbols.

The United States flag and the Liberty Bell stand for

_____

_____

Statue of Liberty

Liberty Bell

Francis Scott Key

Patriotic Songs

We sing songs to show we care about our country. "The Star-Spangled Banner" is an anthem. It is our country's song. It is another name for the United States flag, too.

The song was written by Francis Scott Key. He was a good citizen who contributed to our national identity. Francis Scott Key wrote about how our country is free. He wrote about how our country's people are brave.

It is a patriotic custom to sing our national anthem. It reflects American individualism and freedom. We sing it in many places. We sing it in school. We sing it at sporting events. We sing it at patriotic celebrations and on national holidays, too.

3. **Underline** our country's anthem. **Circle** who wrote it.

The Pledge of Allegiance

We honor our country when we say the Pledge of Allegiance. A pledge is a promise. We face the flag and promise to be loyal. We show that we respect our flag and country, too.

4. **Fill in** the blank. Use the details above to help you.

   The Pledge of Allegiance is a

   promise _____

   _____

   _____

5. Turn and face the flag. Recite the Pledge of Allegiance.

The Declaration
of Independence

United States Papers

The Declaration of Independence is an important paper. Leaders who lived long ago wrote this paper. It helped to make our country free.

Leaders wrote the Constitution of the United States when our country was new. It lists the rights and freedoms of people in our country.

Each year, people celebrate Constitution Day on September 17. This was the day leaders signed the Constitution long ago. Each year, we celebrate American freedom and individualism on this special day.

6. **Underline** what we celebrate on Constitution Day.

The United States Constitution

7. ◎ **Fact and Opinion** **Read** the sentence below.
Write whether it is a fact or an opinion.

The Statue of Liberty is an American symbol.

8. I am a good citizen in my
community when

9. **Turn and talk** to a partner about patriotic customs
and celebrations. **Discuss** how they reflect freedom and
American individualism.

10. **Draw** a picture on a separate piece of paper. Show
how you care about our country. **Write** a sentence that
tells about it.

PEARSON **realize** Go online to access your
interactive digital lesson.

49

Lesson 1   TEKS 13.A

1. What is one daily responsibility of a good citizen in a community?

Lesson 2   TEKS 13.A, 17.C, 18.B

2. Draw two pictures. Show one responsibility you have at home and one you have at school.

3. Read the question and (circle) the best answer.

What is a rule or law that helps you manage conflict at school?

A Wash your hands before you eat.

B Take turns on the swing and slide.

C Throw trash in the trash can.

D Turn out the light when you leave.

4. Look at the words in the box. **Underline** leaders at home. (Circle) leaders at school.

principal	grandfather	teacher
mother	older sister	bus driver
father	crossing guard	librarian

Lesson 5 TEKS 12.B

5. ◎ **Fact and Opinion** Read the sentences below about the roles of public officials. **Underline** the fact. **Circle** the opinion.

A   I think our mayor is a very good leader.

B   The president is the leader of our country.

Lesson 6 TEKS 14.B, 14.C

6. **Complete** the sentence. Use a word from the box.

| pledge | motto | anthem |

"In God We Trust" is a _____

_____

Go online to write and illustrate your own **myStory Book** using the **myStory Ideas** from this chapter.

 THE BIG ?

How do people best cooperate?

TEKS
SS 11.A, 13.A
ELA 17

In this chapter you learned about being a good citizen.

Draw a picture of people in your community who are being good citizens.

PEARSON
realize.   Go online to access your interactive digital lesson.

53

Work in the Community

How do people get what they need?

Draw a picture of yourself doing a job at school or at home.

my Story Video

Texas Essential Knowledge and Skills

7.A Describe ways that families meet basic human needs.

7.B Describe similarities and differences in ways families meet basic human needs.

8.A Identify examples of goods and services in the home, school, and community.

8.B Identify ways people exchange goods and services.

8.C Identify the role of markets in the exchange of goods and services.

9.A Identify examples of people wanting more than they can have.

9.B Explain why wanting more than they can have requires that people make choices.

9.C Identify examples of choices families make when buying goods and services.

10.A Describe the components of various jobs and the characteristics of a job well performed.

10.B Describe how specialized jobs contribute to the production of goods and services.

17.B Obtain information about a topic using a variety of valid visual sources such as pictures, symbols, electronic media, maps, literature, and artifacts.

17.C Sequence and categorize information.

18.A Express ideas orally based on knowledge and experiences.

18.B Create and interpret visual and written material.

19.B Use a decision-making process to identify a situation that requires a decision, gather information, generate options, predict outcomes, take action to implement a decision, and reflect on the effectiveness of that decision.

 # Begin With a Song

Trucks and Buses

Sing to the tune of "On Top of Old Smokey."

Cindy's a plumber.
She unclogs the tub.
She unclogs the sink, too,
And gives it a scrub.

George drives a big truck
With his puppy in back.
George has all the lumber
In one giant stack.

Vocabulary Preview

- needs
- wants
- choice
- scarce
- goods

Identify examples of these words and (circle) them in the picture.

services

producer

consumer

market

job

57

What We Need, What We Want

Envision It!

1 **2**

Look at the places that each have a number.

TEKS
7.A, 7.B, 17.B, 17.C, 18.A, 18.B

There are things people must have to live. There are things people like to have.

People Have Needs

Needs are things we must have to live. Food, water, and clothing are basic human needs. We drink water. Families grow or buy food to eat. We make or buy clothing and **shelter,** or a place to live.

1. **Look** at the picture on this page. **Circle** things that are needs.

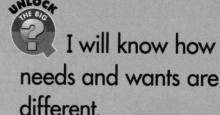
Write the number of the place that matches the items people use there.

People Have Wants

Wants are things we would like to have. We do not need these things to live. A TV is a want. It is fun to watch. It is not something we need to live.

2. **Think** of a need and a want that are not shown in the chart. **Write** the need and want where they belong in the chart.

People Have Needs and Wants	
Needs	**Wants**
food	bike
home	telephone

PEARSON **realize** | Go online to access your interactive digital lesson.

59

Meeting Needs and Wants

All families have the same basic human needs. They need food and water. They need clothing and shelter. People have different wants. They want toys, or cars, or other things.

Families meet their needs in different ways. Some grow their own food. Others sew their own clothing. Some build their own homes. Others have workers build them.

Most people use money to buy the things they need and want. **Money** is coins or bills that are used to buy things. People work to earn money.

3. **Cause and Effect Read** the sentences below. **Circle** the cause.

People need money to buy things.

People earn money when they work.

Got it?

🔺 TEKS 7.A, 7.B, 17.C

4. ⊙**Fact and Opinion Read** the sentence below. **Write** whether it is a fact or an opinion.

We all need food to live.

_____

5. 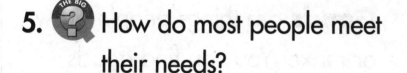 How do most people meet their needs?

 my Story Ideas

_____

_____

_____

6. Draw pictures on separate pieces of paper. Show ways families meet their basic human needs. **Turn and talk** to a partner about your pictures. **Describe** similarities and differences in the ways families meet their needs.

Goods and Services

Mark an X on the people who make things.

TEKS
8.A, 17.B, 17.C, 18.B

Some workers do things for people. Other workers make things. People buy these things to meet their needs.

What Are Goods?

Goods are things people grow or make. You can find goods at home, at school, and in the community. Goods like apples and corn are grown. Goods like toys and beds are made. We use these goods at home.

1. **Circle** the names of home goods in the text above.

You can find goods at school. Desks and paper are some goods you use at school. Rulers and math books are school goods, too. Library books, park benches, and cars are some goods you can find in your community.

2. ◎ **Cause and Effect Read** the sentences below. **Underline** the effect.

Children like to play with toys and games at home and in school.

Workers make toys for children.

What Are Services?

Services are jobs people do to help others. Some service workers help people at home. Gardeners mow lawns. Nurses care for sick people in their homes.

Schools have service workers. Teachers help you learn. Bus drivers drive you to and from school. Coaches show you how to play sports.

Communities have service workers, too. Police and firefighters help keep you safe. Mail carriers bring mail to your home.

3. Name a service worker. **Write** what that person does.

4. ◉ **Compare and Contrast Write** two goods and two services in the chart.

Kinds of Goods and Services	
Goods	**Services**

5. What kind of service would you like to do for other people?

6. Draw a chart on a separate piece of paper. Write the words Home, School, and Community at the top. **Identify** and **write** examples of goods and services people use in each place.

PEARSON realize. Go online to access your interactive digital lesson.

65

Collaboration and Creativity

Decision Making

A decision is a choice made from two or more things. Look at the picture. Read the steps. Think about how the children make a decision.

1. Identify a decision to make.

2. Gather information about it.

3. Name choices.

4. Ask: "Which choice will work the best?"

5. Take action and make a decision.

6. Think about how well your decision worked.

TEKS

SS 17.B Obtain information using visual sources.

SS 19.B Use a decision-making process to identify a situation that requires a decision, gather information, generate options, predict outcomes, take action to implement a decision, and reflect on the effectiveness of that decision.

ELA 14.D Use text features (e.g., illustrations) to locate specific information in text.

1. **Look** at the picture. **Name** a decision that needs to be made.

2. **Draw** a picture. Show one way the children can make a decision. **Tell** why this choice works the best.

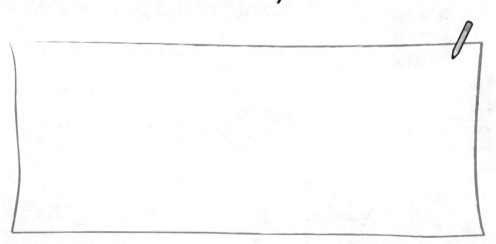

3. **Practice** voting as a way to make a decision. **Choose** a name for a class pet.

PEARSON **realize** Go online to access your interactive digital lesson.

67

Why We Make Choices

Which would you choose to eat?
Mark an *X* on your choice.

TEKS
9.A, 9.B, 9.C, 17.B, 18.A, 18.B

Sometimes we want more than we can have. Then we have to make a choice. We make a **choice** when we pick between two or more things. We pick one thing. We leave the other thing or things.

1. **Look** at the pictures. Which food do you think would be a good choice for dinner? Circle that food.

I will know that people need to make choices when things are scarce.

Vocabulary

choice
scarce

Write why you chose it.

We Choose What to Buy

Sometimes there is not enough of something. When there is not enough of something, it is **scarce.** Money can be scarce. Families may want more than they can have. They may not have enough money to buy everything they want. Then they must make a choice. Look at the picture. This family will choose between buying two goods.

2. ◉ **Cause and Effect**
   <u>Underline</u> the words above that tell why families have to make choices.

PEARSON realize   Go online to access your interactive digital lesson.

69

We Choose Services

People pay for some services. Sometimes we have to make a choice between two services. You may want to take a dance class and a swim class, too. You can not do them both if they are at the same time. Your family may not have money to pay for both classes. You may have to make a choice.

3. Underline the words above that tell why you have to make choices between services.

4. **Cause and Effect** Read the sentences below.
Underline the effect.

Three children want apples for a snack. There is only one small apple. Two children must choose a different snack.

5. Think of a time you had to choose between two things. What did you choose? How did you decide?

my Story Ideas

6. Draw a picture on a separate piece of paper. Show two goods or services you want to have. You can not have both. **Circle** the choice you make. **Explain** why you chose it.

7. Turn and talk to a partner. **Discuss** why wanting more than they can have requires people to make choices.

PEARSON realize Go online to access your interactive digital lesson.

71

Cause and Effect

Tina walked down the street. It started to rain. Tina opened her umbrella.

cause

effect

A cause is what makes something happen. What caused Tina to open her umbrella? It started to rain.

An effect is what happens. What effect did the rain have? Tina opened her umbrella.

Learning Objective

I will know how to identify cause and effect.

TEKS

ELA 4.B Ask relevant questions, seek clarification, and locate facts and details about stories and other texts.
ELA 14.B Identify important facts or details in text.

Read the sentences. Then **look** at the pictures.

Travis made a tower with blocks. His dog ran into the tower. The tower fell.

1. What made the tower fall? **Write** the cause.

_____

_____

2. What happened to the tower? **Write** the effect.

_____

_____

PEARSON realize   Go online to access your interactive digital lesson.

73

Buying and Selling

Look at the boots.

TEKS
8.B, 8.C, 17.B, 18.A, 18.B

People get goods and services in different ways. One way is to trade, or exchange, them. When we **trade,** we give one thing to get something else. We can trade goods we make. We can trade services. We can also trade money for goods and services.

1. **Main Idea and Details**
   Circle the main idea in the text above.

HOME GROWN TOMATOES

FRESH Lemonade

Draw a picture of where you could go to buy the boots.

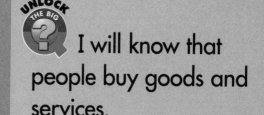
Producers and Consumers

A **producer** grows or makes goods. Bakers are producers. Bakers make bread. Producers may sell the goods they make.

A **consumer** uses goods and services. Consumers buy the bread that bakers make. Producers can be consumers, too. They buy things they need to make goods. Bakers buy flour to make bread.

2. Write what a producer does.

_____

- - - - - - - - - - - - - - - - - - -

PEARSON realize   Go online to access your interactive digital lesson.

75

Markets

Producers take goods and services to markets. A **market** is a place where goods are sold. Services can be sold at a market, too. Consumers buy goods and services there. You can find food, clothes, and toys at markets.

3. (Circle) goods in the picture that are sold at markets.

4. **Main Idea and Details** **Read** the sentences. **Circle** the main idea.

> Producers sell goods and services at markets.
> Bakers are producers. They make goods.
> They sell baked goods at markets.

5. **THE BIG ?** Think of a job as a producer you would like to have. What would you produce?

my Story Ideas

----

6. **Turn and talk** to a partner. **Discuss** the role of markets in the exchange of goods and services.

7. **Draw** a picture on a separate piece of paper. Show ways people exchange goods and services. **Tell** about your picture.

Spending and Saving

Mark an X on each picture that shows what you can do with money.

TEKS
7.A, 7.B, 8.B, 9.A, 9.B, 9.C, 17.B, 18.A, 18.B

Long ago, families met their basic human needs in different ways. People exchanged, or traded, goods and services. A person who fixed chairs needed eggs. A person with a lot of eggs had a broken chair. They traded their goods and services. Then they both got what they needed and wanted.

1. **Look** at the picture of the children holding stickers.

   Circle the goods they are trading.

78

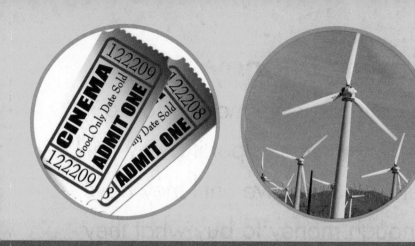

UNLOCK THE BIG ? I will know how people spend and save money.

Vocabulary

save
borrow

Using Money

Families meet their needs by trading. Some families have goods or services to trade. Most families use money to trade. They trade money for goods. They trade money for services. People use money to buy what they need and want.

2. **Underline** words that tell similarities and differences in how families meet their basic human needs.

PEARSON realize. Go online to access your interactive digital lesson.

79

Saving Money

People can save money. To **save** money means to put it away until later. People save until they have enough money to buy what they want and need. Most people save money in a safe place called a bank.

Some people borrow money from a bank. To **borrow** means to take something and promise to return it. People may borrow money to buy what they want and need.

Bea wants more than she can have. She wants a new bike. Bea makes a choice. She rides her old bike. She earns money, too. Bea saves money until she has enough. Then she buys the new bike that she wants!

3. ◎ **Cause and Effect** Circle the reason Bea saves her money.

4. ◉ **Fact and Opinion Read** the sentence below.
Write whether it is a fact or an opinion.

I think it is better to trade with goods than to trade
with money.

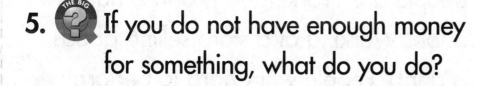

5. If you do not have enough money
for something, what do you do?

my Story Ideas

6. Draw a picture on a separate piece of paper. Show an
example of choices families make when buying goods and
services. **Tell** a partner about your drawing.

7. Turn and talk to a partner. **Discuss** examples of
people wanting more than they can have and the choices
they must make.

PEARSON
realize   Go online to access your
interactive digital lesson.

81

Jobs People Do

Envision It!

Sue feeds the classroom fish. It is one way she helps at school.

People work at jobs. A **job** is the work people do. Working to produce hats is a job. Working at a store selling goods is a job. People work hard to perform, or do, their jobs well.

Many people work to earn money. Some people work only to help others. They do not earn money for their work.

Draw a picture of one way you help at home or at school.

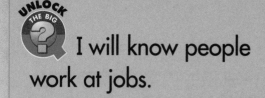
Jobs at Home

People do jobs at home to help their families. One job is to keep your room clean. Another job is to take care of a pet. We are happy when we do a good job. Other people are happy, too!

Some jobs people do at home earn money. People can make things to sell. Some people sew clothing. They sell the clothing to earn money.

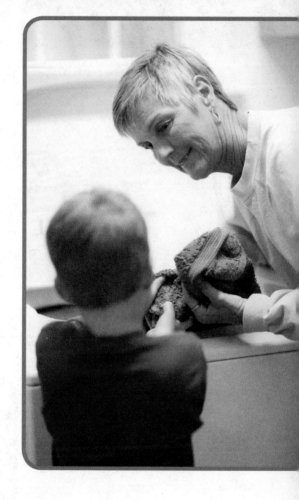

1. ◉ **Main Idea and Details** Circle the main idea above. **Underline** two details.

PEARSON realize. Go online to access your interactive digital lesson.

83

Jobs at School

People have jobs at school. They want to help children. They work hard to do their job well. Teachers and principals help children learn. Cooks work to feed children. Bus drivers take children to school. Crossing guards help children cross the street safely. These workers produce services.

Children work hard at school, too. They listen. They ask questions. They learn. They want to do their best.

2. **Underline** service jobs people have at school.

Different Jobs

People work at different jobs.
Many people are needed to do
some jobs. It takes many people
to make a car or build a house.
It takes many people to build a
school, mall, or airport, too.

Some people use tools to do
their jobs. A painter uses a
brush as a tool. A builder uses
a hammer. A baker uses a
mixer and a rolling pin. A writer
uses paper and a pencil. A
writer uses a computer, too.

3. **Look** at the workers in each
   picture. **Circle** people using
   tools.

Producing Goods and Services

There are specialized jobs that produce goods. Some people make games. Each worker makes a part of the game. Everyone contributes to its production.

There are jobs that produce services. Washing cars is a service. Some people wash cars. Other people dry cars with clean towels. There are people who wash and dry dogs, too! They are called dog groomers.

4. Fill in the blanks using details above.

Some people produce goods by

_____

Some people produce services by

_____

5. ◉ **Cause and Effect Read** the sentences below.
   (Circle) the cause. **Underline** the effect.

   Most people work at jobs.

   They are happy when they do their jobs well.

6. ❓ What different jobs do people
   have in your community?

7. **Draw** a job you perform, or do, well. Use a separate
   piece of paper. **Write** a sentence telling about it.

8. **Turn and talk** to a partner. Take turns naming goods
   and services. **Describe** how specialized jobs contribute to
   the production of each good or service.

PEARSON realize Go online to access your interactive digital lesson.

87

Lesson 1 TEKS 7.A

1. **Write** *want* or *need* under each picture.

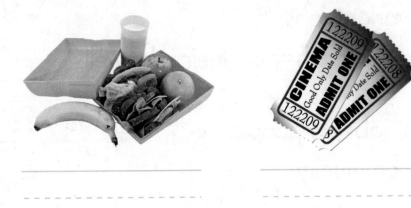

_____

_____

Lesson 2 🦫 TEKS 8.A, 17.C

2. **Look** at the words in the box. Each one is a good. **Write** the words where they belong in the chart.

slides   toys   backpacks   beds   cars   desks

Home	School	Community

Lesson 3  TEKS 9.B, 9.C

3. Circle three items families need and must choose first when money is scarce.

clothing   toy   movie ticket

bike   food   doll

TV   computer   shelter

Lesson 4 TEKS 18.B

4. Which picture shows how people trade for goods? Circle it.

Lesson 5 ⬥ TEKS 9.B, 9.C

5. **Cause and Effect Read** the sentences below. Circle the cause. **Underline** the effect.

Vijay wants to buy a new basketball and new sneakers. He makes a choice. Vijay earns money and buys a new basketball.

Lesson 6 ⬥ TEKS 10.B

6. **Read** the question and circle the best answer.

Which is a job that produces a service at school?

A fold clothes

B rake leaves

C cook food

D make the bed

Go online to write and illustrate your own **myStory Book** using the **myStory Ideas** from this chapter.

THE BIG ? How do people get what they need?

TEKS
SS 18.B
ELA 17

In this chapter you have learned about how people work for what they need or want.

Draw a picture of a job you would like to do when you grow up.

PEARSON
realize · · · Go online to access your interactive digital lesson.

91

Looking at Our World

 my Story Spark

What is the world like?

Think of a place where you like to play outdoors. **Draw** what you see there.

my Story Video

⭐ Texas Essential Knowledge and Skills

4.A Locate places using the four cardinal directions.

4.B Describe the location of self and objects relative to other locations in the classroom and school.

5.A Create and use simple maps such as maps of the home, classroom, school, and community.

5.B Locate the community, Texas, and the United States on maps and globes.

6.A Identify and describe the physical characteristics of place such as landforms, bodies of water, natural resources, and weather.

6.B Identify examples of and uses for natural resources in the community, state, and nation.

6.C Identify and describe how the human characteristics of place such as shelter, clothing, food, and activities are based upon geographic location.

17.B Obtain information about a topic using a variety of valid visual sources such as pictures, symbols, electronic media, maps, literature, and artifacts.

17.C Sequence and categorize information.

18.A Express ideas orally based on knowledge and experiences.

18.B Create and interpret visual and written material.

 Begin With a Song

Show You Care

by Emily Sasaki

Sing to the tune of "Yankee Doodle."

You may live upon the plains
Or near a hill or lake.
Show you care about the earth.
There are simple steps to take!

Care for land and wildlife, too.
Let's take care of our nation.
Keep our air and water clean
And practice conservation!

Vocabulary Preview

map

globe

mountain

desert

ocean

ZOO

Pacific
Ocean

Atlantic
Ocean

Reduce
Waste

Identify examples of these words and (**circle**) them in the picture.

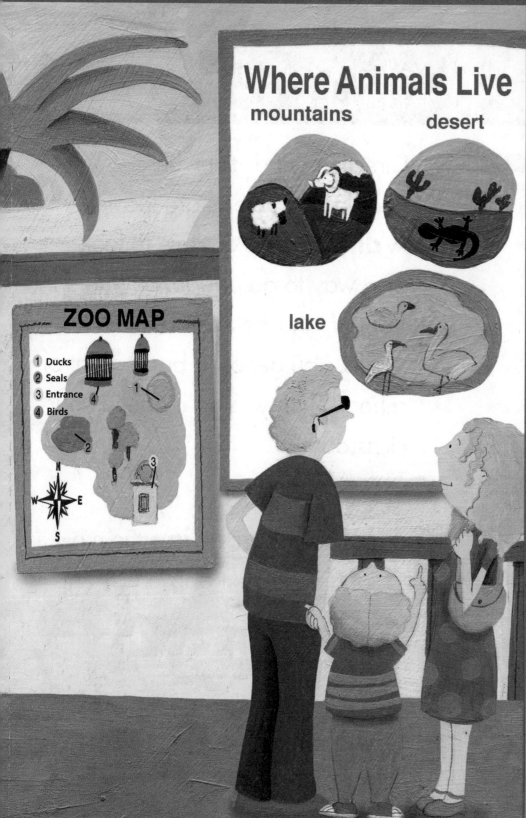

Where Animals Live

mountains

desert

lake

ZOO MAP

1 Ducks
2 Seals
3 Entrance
4 Birds

N
W E
S

lake

continent

reduce

reuse

recycle

Where Things Are Located

Envision It!

Mark an *X* on the chair next to the teacher's desk.

TEKS
4.A, 4.B, 5.A, 17.B, 18.B

Direction words tell where people and objects are located. A **direction** is a place to look or a way to go. *Inside, outside, in front of,* and *behind* are direction words. You get off a bus in front of school. Then you go inside to your classroom!

1. ◎ **Main Idea and Details Underline** the main idea in the text above.

HURSTON
ELEMENTARY SCHOOL

BUS

UNLOCK THE BIG ?

I will know that directions help us locate places and things.

Vocabulary

direction

map

You are in front of the bookcase. What is to its left? Circle it.

Where Places Are

We can use direction words to say where places are. In the picture, the firehouse is to the left of the brown house. The word *left* tells us where to look.

2. **Draw** a tree to the right of the brown house.
   Draw yourself in front of the firehouse.

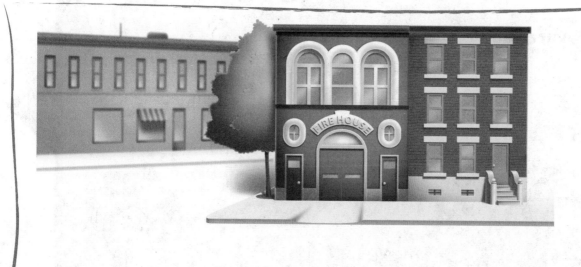

Directions on a Map

A **map** is a drawing of a place. It shows where things are. Maps use the directions north, south, east, and west.

Look at the map below. Put your finger on the school. Move your finger to the arrow marked West. The playground is west of the school.

3. Circle what is east of the playground on the map.

4. ◎ **Main Idea and Details Read** the sentences below. Circle the main idea.

> I can use direction words to say where I am located. I am behind the school. I am sitting near a tree.

5. ❓ **Think** of a place where you learn.   my **Story Ideas**
   Write where it is. Use direction words.

_____

_____

_____

_____

6. Use a separate piece of paper. **List** three places or objects in your school. **Describe** the location of the places or objects relative to other locations in the school. Then share descriptions with a classmate. **Identify** the places from your partner's descriptions.

7. Draw a picture on a separate piece of paper. Show yourself in the classroom. **Describe** your location relative to other locations in the classroom and school.

Parts of a Map

A map has many parts. The title tells what the map shows. The title of this map is Downtown. The compass rose shows cardinal directions. Points show N for north, S for south, E for east, and W for west. Map symbols are pictures that stand for real things. The legend tells what the symbols mean. The library symbol on the map shows where the library is.

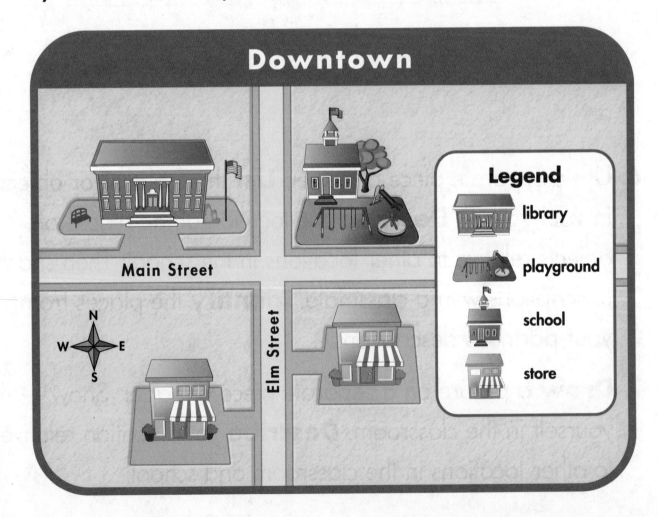

Downtown

Main Street

Elm Street

N
W   E
S

Legend

library

playground

school

store

TEKS

SS 4.A Locate places using the four cardinal directions.

SS 5.A Create and use maps of the home, classroom, school, and community.

SS 17.B Obtain information using visual sources such as maps.

SS 18.B Create and interpret visual material.

ELA 15.B Explain the meaning of signs and symbols (e.g., map features).

1. **Circle** the compass rose on the map below.

2. **Underline** the symbol for the firehouse on the map and in the legend.

3. **Create** a map of your home or school on a separate piece of paper. Think about what details to show. Include a compass rose, symbols, and a legend. Give your map a title.

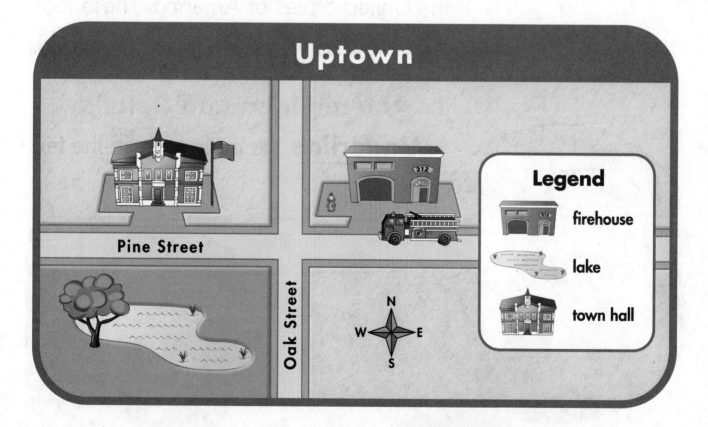

PEARSON realize Go online to access your interactive digital lesson.

101

Maps and Globes

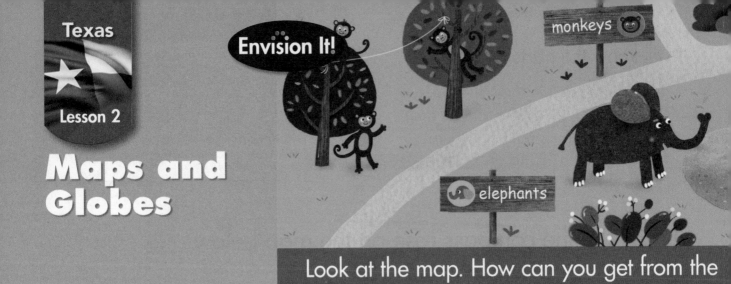

Look at the map. How can you get from the elephants to the lions?

TEKS
5.A, 5.B, 17.B, 18.B

Maps and globes are tools that help us locate places. We use them to get from place to place in our community and in the great state of Texas, too. These tools show us where we live in our country, the United States of America. These tools also show us where we live in the world.

1. ◎ **Main Idea and Details**
Underline the main idea in the text above.

Zoo

lions

Draw a line on the path to show how to get there.

Globes

Earth is where we live. It is round, like a ball. A **globe** is a round model of Earth. It shows all the land and water on Earth. The blue part shows water. The brown and green parts show land. Globes show countries and states like the United States and Texas. They show cities, too.

2. **Look** at the pictures on both pages. Draw a ⬭circle⬭ around tools that help you find places.

PEARSON realize Go online to access your interactive digital lesson.

103

Maps

Maps also show land and water, but maps are flat. Maps can show places like states and towns.

Maps can show places like classrooms, too. A classroom map can show objects like desks and chairs. You can use the map to describe the relative location of the bookcase to the table. The bookcase is south of the table.

Maps may show cardinal directions. Points or arrows show north, south, east, and west.

3. **Fill in** the blank with a cardinal direction word. Use the map to **describe** the location of the desk relative to the bookcase.

_____

The desk is _____ of the bookcases.

North

Our Classroom

West

East

South

Legend

■ desk   ▪ chair

▬ bookcase   ■ table

Finding Small Places on a Map

We can use maps to locate small places. The map at the right shows a school. It also shows places inside the school, like classrooms and the lunchroom. You can use the map to describe the location of places and objects in the school relative to other locations. You can describe the nurse's office as east of the classrooms. You can describe the jumprope in the gym as south of the desks in the classrooms.

Our School

North

West

East

South

LEGEND
- classroom
- lunchroom
- gym
- nurse's office
- —— walls

Some maps have a legend, or key. The **legend** tells what the symbols on the map mean. For example, the gym symbol on the legend shows you which room is the gym on the map.

4. **Look** at the map. **Draw** a route from the gym to the lunchroom.

Finding Large Places on a Map

We can use maps to find large places. The map below shows all 50 states in our country. It also shows Washington, D.C. This is our nation's capital.

Look at the legend. It shows a star for the national capital. Find the star on the map. The star marks where Washington, D.C. is.

5. **Look** at the map below. **Mark** an X on Texas. **Circle** the United States.

North

The United States of America

West

East

South

Legend
★ national capital

Got it?

6.  **Compare and Contrast** How are maps and globes alike? How are they different?

Alike

_____

- -

_____

Different

_____

- -

_____

7. Think about a map of your community. What are some places you would include in your map?

 **my Story Ideas**

_____

- -

_____

8. **Spin** a globe. When it stops, **locate** and point to the United States. Then **locate** Texas and your community, too.

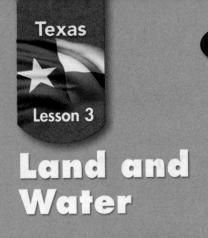

Texas

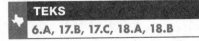

Lesson 3

Land and Water

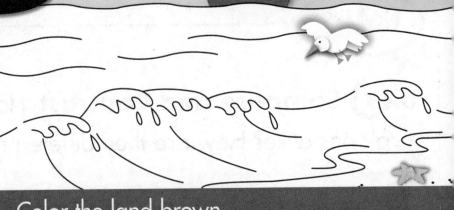

Color the land brown.
Color the water blue.

TEKS
6.A, 17.B, 17.C, 18.A, 18.B

Places on Earth have things from nature, such as land and water. They also have things people have made, such as houses and roads.

Physical Characteristics

Things from nature are the physical characteristics of a place. Physical characteristics include land and water.

1. **Look** at the picture. **Identify** and (circle) land. **Draw** an X on water.

UNLOCK THE BIG ?

I will know about different forms of land and water on Earth.

Vocabulary

mountain   ocean
hill   lake
desert   river

Landforms

Different kinds of land are called landforms. Landforms are one example of physical characteristics of place. A **mountain** is the highest kind of land. A **hill** is higher than flat land but not as high as a mountain. A **desert** is land that is very dry.

2. **Draw** a line to connect each landform picture to its name in the text.

Bodies of Water

There are different bodies of water. Bodies of water are also physical characteristics of place. An **ocean** is a very large body of water. Ocean water is salty. A **lake** has land on all sides. Lakes are smaller than oceans. A **river** is long. Rivers flow toward a lake or an ocean. The water in most lakes and rivers is not salty.

3. Draw a line to connect each picture to its name in the text.

Got it?

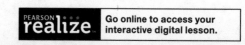

4. ◉ **Compare and Contrast Write** one way lakes and oceans are alike. **Write** one way they are different.

Alike

_____

_____

Different

_____

_____

5. ? What kind of landform or body of water is near your community?

my Story Ideas

_____

_____

6. **Draw** a picture on a separate piece of paper. Show a landform or body of water where you live. Trade pictures with a partner. **Identify** and **describe** what your partner drew. Use your vocabulary words.

Continents and Oceans

This is a picture of the United States. It is taken from space.

TEKS
5.B, 6.A, 17.B, 18.A, 18.B

A map of the world can show all of Earth. The map below shows all of Earth's land and water. Most of Earth is covered by water. Land and water are physical characteristics of place.

The World

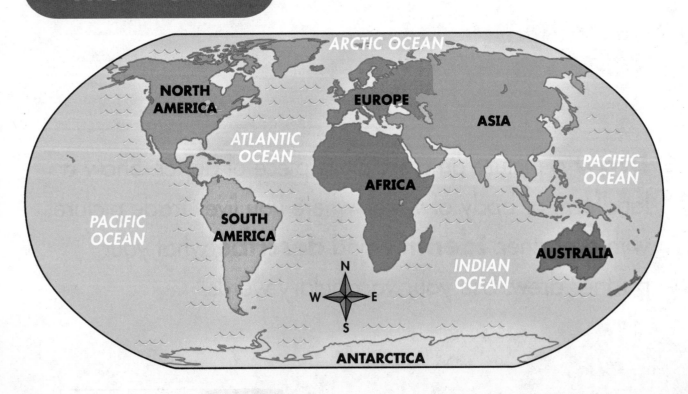

ARCTIC OCEAN

NORTH AMERICA

EUROPE

ASIA

ATLANTIC OCEAN

AFRICA

PACIFIC OCEAN

PACIFIC OCEAN

SOUTH AMERICA

INDIAN OCEAN

AUSTRALIA

N
W E
S

ANTARCTICA

Write what the green and brown areas in the picture show.

Continents and Oceans

A **continent** is a large area of land. There are seven continents on Earth. We live on the continent of North America.

There are four large bodies of water on Earth called oceans. North America touches three oceans. It touches the Atlantic Ocean on the east. It touches the Pacific Ocean on the west. It touches the Arctic Ocean to the north.

1. ◎ **Main Idea and Details**
   Circle the main idea above.

PEARSON realize. Go online to access your interactive digital lesson.

113

North America

The United States is a country on the continent of North America. Texas is located in the United States. Your community is located in Texas. Canada and Mexico are also countries in North America. Canada is north of the United States. Mexico is south of the United States.

2. Locate bodies of water on the map. **Circle** the Arctic Ocean, Pacific Ocean, and Atlantic Ocean. **Underline** the Gulf of Mexico.

Got it?

TEKS 5.B, 6.A, 18.A

3. ◉ **Main Idea and Details Read** the sentences below. **Circle** the main idea. **Underline** the details.

> Earth has many kinds of land and water. It has seven continents. It has four oceans.

4. On what continent is your community located?

my Story Ideas

- -

5. Locate the United States on a globe. Use your finger to trace a circle around the globe back to the United States. **Turn and talk** to a classmate. **Tell** about the oceans and continents your circle crossed.

Our Environment

Circle things that do not belong on a sunny beach.

TEKS
6.A, 6.B, 6.C, 17.B, 18.A, 18.B

Earth is our home. We use things on Earth to help us live.

Natural Resources

A resource is something we can use. Natural resources come from nature. We use water to drink, cook, and wash. We grow food in soil. We use trees to make things.

Natural resources are physical characteristics of places. Some places have many of these resources.

1. **Underline** natural resources.

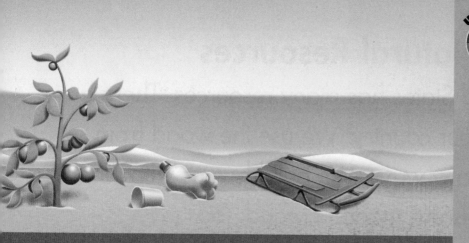

UNLOCK THE BIG ? I will know how weather and natural resources affect the way we live.

Vocabulary

weather   reuse
reduce   recycle

Caring for Earth

We can take care of our natural resources. When we **reduce**, we use less of something. You reduce the amount of water you use when you turn off the tap while you brush your teeth.

When we **reuse,** we use something again. You can reuse a cloth lunch bag day after day.

When we **recycle,** we take one thing and make it into something new. Old tires are recycled into a soft ground cover for playgrounds.

2. **Underline** ways to care for Earth.

Using Natural Resources

The United States has many resources. There are forests in our country. We use the wood from trees in many ways. We build homes with wood. Our pencils are made of wood, too.

Texas is a big state with many resources. Oil from under the ground is used for fuel. The soil is good in many parts of Texas. Farmers grow corn and wheat. We eat corn on the cob. We use wheat to make bread and pasta.

Plants and animals are natural resources, too. Texas ranchers raise cattle. Fishing communities catch fish and shrimp in the water of the Gulf of Mexico. We put shrimp in our tacos!

3. **Circle** natural resources. **Underline** ways they are used.

Weather

Weather is what it is like outside at a certain time. Weather is a physical characteristic of place. It is not the same in all places. Some places have hot weather. Some places have cold weather. Places can have dry, wet, or snowy weather.

Homes can keep us warm or cool. The weather helps us choose what kind of home to build. The home in the top picture has thick walls. They keep the inside cool. The home in the bottom picture has a sloped roof. It lets snow slide off.

4. **Fill in** the blank using the details above to help you.

Rain is a kind of
_____
_____

People and Places

People change places. They build homes and roads. Things people make are human characteristics of place. So are clothing, food, and activities. These things are different in different geographic locations.

People who live in cold places need warm clothing. People in warm places need light clothing.

Different trees and plants grow in different places. People use different materials to build homes. They eat different foods.

5. Circle an activity you would do in a warm place.

6. 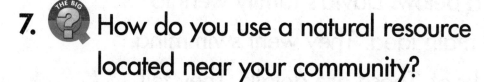 **Cause and Effect** What kind of weather would cause you to wear a coat?

_____

_____

_____

7. How do you use a natural resource located near your community?

_____

_____

8. Draw a picture of an outdoor activity in your community. Use a separate piece of paper. Share your drawing with a classmate. **Identify** human characteristics of place in your classmate's drawing. **Describe** how these things are based upon your geographic location.

9. Interview a friend or family member about a place in Texas. **Obtain** information about food, clothing, and shelter. **Describe** how these things are based upon geographic location.

Main Idea and Details

Every story has a main idea. This is the most important, or big, idea. Details tell more about the main idea. The main idea of a paragraph is often the first sentence.

Look at the postcard below. David's family went to the lake. This is the main idea. They went swimming. They went out in a boat. These are details. They tell more about the main idea.

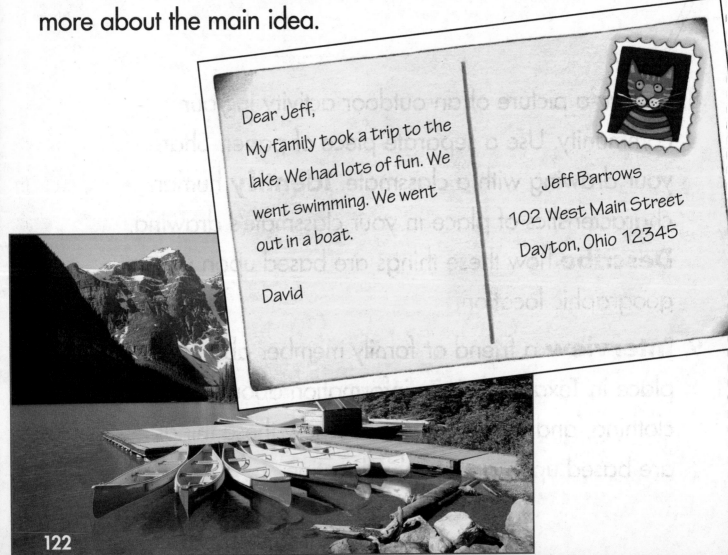

Dear Jeff,

My family took a trip to the lake. We had lots of fun. We went swimming. We went out in a boat.

David

Jeff Barrows
102 West Main Street
Dayton, Ohio 12345

TEKS

SS 6.C Identify and describe how the human characteristics of place such as activities are based upon geographic location.

ELA 4.B Ask relevant questions and locate facts and details about texts.

ELA 14.A Restate the main idea.

ELA 14.B Identify important facts or details in text.

1. **Read** the postcard from Jackie below.

2. **Circle** the main idea. **Underline** the details.

Dear Grandma,

We went to visit Aunt Lexie in the mountains. We rode sleds. We made snowballs. It was cold, but fun!

Jackie

Mrs. Mary Munoz
3002 West First Avenue
Tampa, FL 12345

PEARSON realize Go online to access your interactive digital lesson.

123

Getting From Here to There

Envision It!

Circle the pictures that show ways you have used to go places.

TEKS
4.A, 5.B, 17.C, 18.B

Think of a glass of orange juice. It takes many steps to get the juice to your glass. Workers pick the oranges. Trucks move them to a factory. Workers make the oranges into juice. They put the juice into bottles. Trucks move the bottles to stores. Then you can buy the juice and pour it into a glass.

124

Transportation

Transportation is the way goods and people move from place to place. Trucks, airplanes, and ships are kinds of transportation. Trains, buses, and bikes are kinds of transportation, too.

We use transportation to go places. Sellers use it to move goods to stores. Buyers use it to go to stores to buy goods like orange juice.

1. Write words to finish the sentence.

I use transportation when I go to

_____

PEARSON realize. Go online to access your interactive digital lesson.

125

Communication

You can communicate with people who live far away. To **communicate** is to give and get information. You can write a letter. You can use a computer to send an e-mail. You can use a telephone to have a conversation.

2. ◉ **Main Idea and Details**
   Circle the main idea in the paragraph above. **Underline** detail sentences.

3. ⊙ **Compare and Contrast** **Write** the words from the box where they belong on the chart.

| truck | telephone | computer | bus |

Transportation and Communication	
Transportation	**Communication**

4. ❓ What types of transportation do you use in your community?

my Story Ideas

_____

_____

5. **Locate** your community on a map of Texas. Choose another place in Texas to visit. **Explain** how you can go there. **Tell** what transportation you can use and what direction you will go.

Lesson 1 🏴 TEKS 4.A, 5.A

1. Look at the map below. Circle things that are north of Main Street.

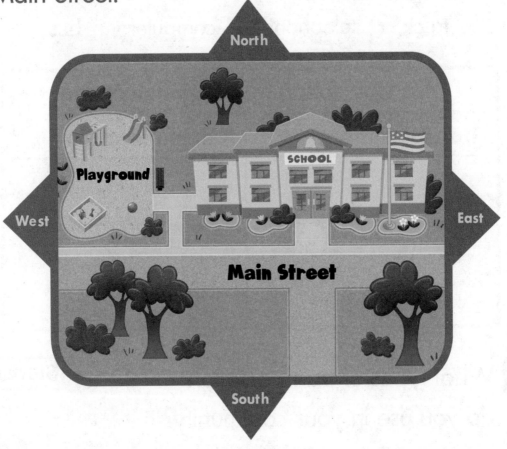

Lesson 2 🏴 TEKS 5.A

2. Look at the map above. **Read** the question and circle the best answer.

What is located west of the school?

A Main Street

C the flag pole

B the playground

D one tree

3. **Look** at the map. **Mark** an X on natural resources. **Circle** something made by people using natural resources. Tell how people use each resource.

Uptown

Pine Street

4. North America is on the top left. **Circle** the United States. **Mark** an X to show where Texas is located.

The World

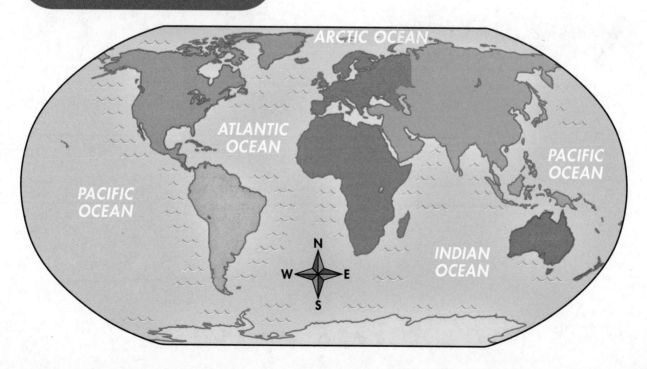

ARCTIC OCEAN

ATLANTIC OCEAN

PACIFIC OCEAN

PACIFIC OCEAN

INDIAN OCEAN

N
W E
S

Lesson 5 🔹 TEKS 6.C

5. What would you wear outside if you lived in a cold place?

_____

_____

_____

Lesson 6 🔹 TEKS 18.B

6. ◎ **Main Idea and Details Read** the sentences below. **Circle** the main idea. **Write** one detail sentence.

There are many kinds of transportation. Trucks are often used to move goods. Buses are often used to move people.

_____

_____

_____

Go online to write and illustrate your own **myStory Book** using the **myStory Ideas** from this chapter.

What is the world like?

TEKS

SS 5.A

ELA 17

Draw a map of a real place you know well. Choose one of these places: your home, your classroom, your school, or your community.

PEARSON realize   Go online to access your interactive digital lesson.

131

Traditions We Share

my Story Spark

THE BIG ? How is culture shared?

my Story Video

Draw a picture of you and your family. Show a favorite activity you do together.

★ Texas Essential Knowledge and Skills

1.A Describe the origins of customs, holidays, and celebrations of the community, state, and nation such as San Jacinto Day, Independence Day, and Veterans Day.

1.B Compare the observance of holidays and celebrations, past and present.

2.A Identify contributions of historical figures, including Sam Houston, George Washington, Abraham Lincoln, and Martin Luther King Jr., who have influenced the community, state, and nation.

2.B Identify historical figures such as Alexander Graham Bell, Thomas Edison, Garrett Morgan, and Richard Allen, and other individuals who have exhibited individualism and inventiveness.

2.C Compare the similarities and differences among the lives and activities of historical figures and other individuals who have influenced the community, state, and nation.

6.C Identify and describe how the human characteristics of place such as shelter, clothing, food, and activities are based upon geographic location.

7.B Describe similarities and differences in ways families meet basic human needs.

13.A Identify characteristics of good citizenship, including truthfulness, justice, equality, respect for oneself and others, responsibility in daily life, and participation in government by educating oneself about the issues, respectfully holding public officials to their word, and voting.

13.B Identify historical figures such as Benjamin Franklin, Francis Scott Key, and Eleanor Roosevelt who have exemplified good citizenship.

13.C Identify other individuals who exemplify good citizenship.

15.A Describe and explain the importance of various beliefs, customs, language, and traditions of families and communities.

15.B Explain the way folktales and legends such as Aesop's fables reflect beliefs, customs, language, and traditions of communities.

17.B Obtain information about a topic using a variety of valid visual sources such as pictures, symbols, electronic media, maps, literature, and artifacts.

17.C Sequence and categorize information.

18.A Express ideas orally based on knowledge and experiences.

18.B Create and interpret visual and written material.

♪ Begin With a Song

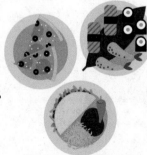

Explore With Me!

Sing to the tune of "Hush, Little Baby."

Travel the world. Explore with me.

There are so many things to do and see.

There are people we will meet.

There are new foods we will eat.

We'll take a boat, a bus, and a train.

We'll fly around the world in a great
    big plane.

We'll learn many things we want to know.

We'll tell all about each place we go.

PEARSON realize. Go online to access your interactive digital lesson.

133

Vocabulary Preview

culture

celebrate

custom

hero

shelter

CULTURAL DAY CELEBRATION

TRY THAI
อาหาร

Identify examples of these words and (circle) them in the picture.

tradition

president

holiday

family

language

What Is Culture?

Envision It!

What is the same about these pictures? **Write** about it.

TEKS
6.C, 7.B, 15.A, 17.B, 18.A, 18.B

There are many families living around the world. All families have the same basic human needs. They need food, clothing, and **shelter,** or a home. Families in different places meet their needs in different ways depending on their geographic location.

1. **Look** at the pictures. **Circle** what is similar about what the children are doing in each picture. **Mark an X** on what is different about how they are doing it.

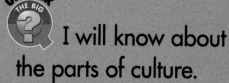
Vocabulary

shelter
culture
language

Different Cultures

Culture is the way a group of people live. There are many different cultures. Each culture has its own music, dance, and art. Each has its own religion, beliefs, and language, too. **Language** is the words we speak.

2. **Look** at the pictures. **Write** one way these cultures are similar, based on what you know.

PEARSON realize   Go online to access your interactive digital lesson.

137

What We Eat

Each culture has its own kinds of food. What we eat is based on our geographic location. How we eat our food is based on where we live, too. Many people use forks to eat their food. Other people use chopsticks. There are some foods that people eat using their hands.

In our country, we can eat food from many cultures. We use forks and chopsticks. We use our hands, too!

3. **Circle** foods you eat with your hands.

What We Wear

Clothing is a part of every culture. Our clothes are different. They are alike, too. We have clothes for school, work, and play. We have clothes for special days.

What people wear is based on their geographic location. In hot places, people wear clothes that keep them cool. In cold places, they wear clothes that keep them warm.

4.  **Main Idea and Details**
   Circle the main idea in the second paragraph. **Underline** two details.

Where We Live

All people need shelter. How people build their shelter is based on geographic location. In hot places, homes are made to keep heat out. In cold places, homes are made to keep heat in.

Some homes are made of stone, mud, or brick. Other homes are made of wood from trees.

Some homes are made for one family. Other homes are made for many families.

5. **Look** at the pictures.
   Write one way these homes are different.

   _____
   _____
   _____
   _____

6. ◎ **Compare and Contrast** What is similar about human needs in all cultures? What is different?

_____

_____

_____

7. ❓ What is one thing you would like to ⓜ Story Ideas tell someone about your culture?

_____

_____

_____

8. **Cut out** magazine pictures that show shelter, food, clothing, and activities. **Glue** them on poster paper. **Turn and talk** to a partner about the shelter, food, clothing, and activities you chose. **Describe** how they are based on geographic location, or where people live.

Families Are Alike and Different

Envision It!

Here are two different families.

TEKS
7.B, 15.A, 17.B, 18.B

A **family** is a group of people who live together. A family may be small. A family may be large.

All families are the same in some ways. The people in a family share the same culture. They take care of each other. They each have responsibilities in their family.

Family Customs

Families have many customs. A **custom** is the way people usually do something.

Draw a picture of your family.

Vocabulary

family

custom

tradition

Families communicate in their own language. Some families speak more than one language. Many families share customs about their beliefs.

The different customs families have make each family special. Sharing a meal is an important custom in many families.

1. **Circle** a custom shown in this picture.

PEARSON **realize** Go online to access your interactive digital lesson.

143

Families Share Culture

Families share their culture with their community. The songs, dances, and foods that communities share are traditions. A **tradition** is a way to do something that people pass down over time.

Look at the picture. A family owns this market. Here, they sell foods from their culture. When people buy and eat these foods, they share the family's culture.

2. ◎ **Compare and Contrast** How is this market like one in your community? How is it different?

3. ⊙ **Sequence** **Write** one sentence about a food custom you share with your family. **Tell** what you do first.

First, we _____

_____

4. ❓ What is a tradition you share with your family?

my Story Ideas

_____

5. **Draw** a picture. Use a separate piece of paper. Show how you share a custom or tradition with your family and community. **Tell** a classmate about your picture.

6. **Turn and talk** to a partner. **Discuss** different languages spoken in your family and community. **Talk** about different beliefs, too.

PEARSON **realize** | Go online to access your interactive digital lesson.

145

Sharing Our Cultures

Envision It!

Look at the children playing their favorite game.

TEKS
15.A, 17.B, 17.C, 18.B
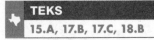

Children from other countries speak different languages. They have different customs and traditions. Meet some children from other countries.

Meet Choon-Hee

Hello! I am Choon-Hee from South Korea. When I get home from school, I leave my shoes by my front door. This is an old custom in my country. Next, I play music. Last, I set the table. We use chopsticks when we eat.

1. **Sequence Write** 1, 2, or 3 by the sentence that tells what Choon-Hee does first, next, and last after school.

146

Draw a game that you like to play.

Vocabulary

fiesta

Meet Pedro

Hello! My name is Pedro. I live with my family in Mexico. My home is by the ocean. I like to swim. I like to play football. You call it soccer.

On Saturday, there will be a **fiesta,** or holiday, in my town. It is a fun tradition. We will hear music. We will eat good food. We will play games and have fun.

2. **Write** one thing Pedro does that you would like to do.

_____

Meet Hawa

I am Hawa from Mali. I live with my family. My mother is a teacher. One day, I want to be a teacher.

My family gets up at 7 o'clock. We eat breakfast. Then I walk to school. It takes 20 minutes to get there.

My class meets on the playground. We raise our country's flag. It is a custom to sing our country's song.

3. **Underline** something that you and Hawa both do at school.

Meet Kurt

Guten Tag (GOO tun tahg)! That means "hello" in German. I live in a big city in Germany. I have a computer that I use at school. I also use it to write to friends far away.

4. Circle the words that mean "hello" in German.

5. ⊙ **Compare and Contrast** **Write** one way you and the children in this lesson are similar. **Write** one way you are different.

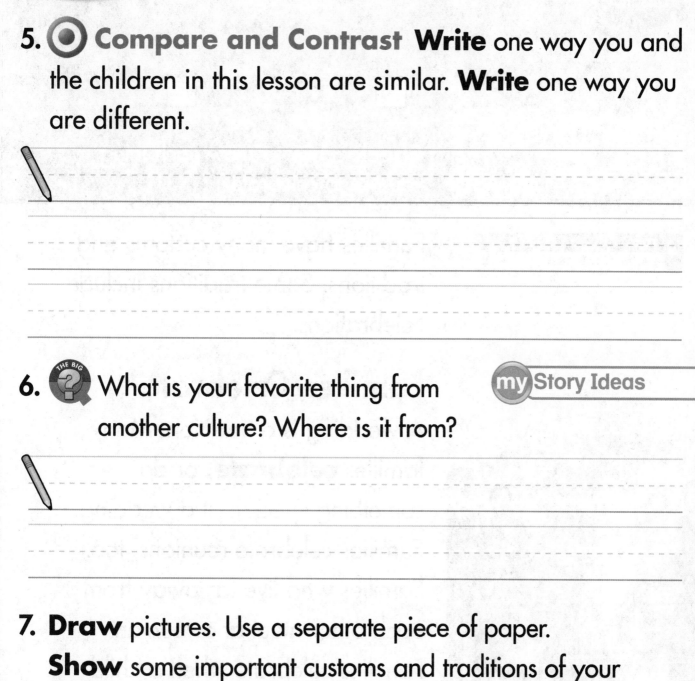

6. **What is your favorite thing from another culture? Where is it from?**

my Story Ideas

7. **Draw** pictures. Use a separate piece of paper. **Show** some important customs and traditions of your family or community. **Write** a sentence about each one.

PEARSON
realize   Go online to access your interactive digital lesson.

149

What Are Our Celebrations?

Envision It!

Check a box to show each thing you use to celebrate.

TEKS
1.A, 15.A, 17.B, 18.B

Families have many customs and traditions. Some traditions include celebrations.

Families Celebrate

A wedding is a tradition. Many families **celebrate,** or do something special, at a wedding. Families celebrate reunions, too. Families who live far away from each other meet at a reunion. Families celebrate when a child finishes school, too.

1. ◎ **Main Idea and Details**
   (Circle) the main idea on this page.
   Underline one detail.

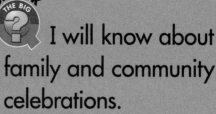
How We Celebrate

Many families celebrate holidays with traditions. A **holiday** is a special day. Some holidays honor people. Other holidays honor religious beliefs and traditions. Christmas, Passover, Eid al-Fitr, and Kwanzaa are some holidays.

How do families celebrate holidays? They may eat special foods. They may light candles. They may decorate their homes or give gifts.

2. **Write** the name of a holiday that honors your family's beliefs.

_____

PEARSON realize™ — Go online to access your interactive digital lesson.

151

Community Celebrations

Many communities celebrate their cultures. Some communities have parades. People play music. They dance. They eat special foods.

In some celebrations, people tell stories. Some stories are about important people. Others have their origins, or beginnings, in famous events from the past. One important celebration in Texas is San Jacinto Day. On this day, people remember when Texas won its freedom from Mexico. On the Independence Day holiday, people remember that the United States, our nation, won its freedom from England. Many communities have their own customs to celebrate their origins.

3. **Underline** why people celebrate San Jacinto Day.

4.  **Compare and Contrast** **Write** one way many holidays are alike. **Write** one way they are different.

Alike: _____

_____

Different: _____

_____

5. **What is a community celebration where you live?**

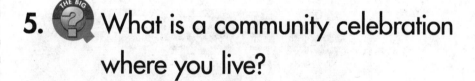

my Story Ideas

_____

_____

6. **Write** a list of holidays your family celebrates. Use a separate piece of paper. **Turn and talk** to a partner about your family celebrations. **Discuss** why your customs, traditions, and beliefs are important to you.

7. **Draw** a picture of how you celebrate San Jacinto Day. **Tell** about your picture.

PEARSON realize   Go online to access your interactive digital lesson.

153

Compare and Contrast

We compare to show how things are alike or the same. We contrast to show how things are different or not the same.

Look at the pictures on this page. Then read about where Jin and Matt live. How are their homes alike? How are they different?

Jin's home is made of wood. It has five rooms. One family lives here.

Matt's home is made of brick. It has five rooms. Many families live here.

Alike Each home has five rooms.

Different Jin's home is made for one family. Matt's home is made for many families.

Learning Objective

I will know how to compare and contrast things.

TEKS

SS 7.B Describe similarities and differences in ways families meet basic human needs.

ELA 4.B Locate facts and details about stories and other texts.

Jin goes to school. She wears a uniform. Jin likes to learn about science.

Matt goes to school. He wears jeans and a shirt. Matt likes to learn about math.

1. Write one way that Jin and Matt are alike.

_____

2. Write one way that Jin and Matt are different.

_____

_____

PEARSON **realize** Go online to access your interactive digital lesson.

155

Envision It!

Circle ways people help each other.

TEKS
2.B, 2.C, 13.A, 13.B, 13.C, 17.B, 18.B

Many people **contribute** to, or help, our country.

Helping Others

Good citizens help our country. Eleanor Roosevelt was a good citizen. She worked to help women, children, and the poor. These people did not have equal rights. She helped to write an important paper about these rights.

THE UNIVERSAL DECLARATION OF **Human Rights**

1. ◉ **Main Idea and Details** **Circle** the main idea on this page. **Underline** two details.

Sharing Ideas

Another way to help our country is to share ideas. Richard Allen lived in Texas. He had good ideas. He designed and built houses and bridges.

He learned about issues in the state and became a leader in government. His activities showed his individualism when he acted on his beliefs to help others. Like Eleanor Roosevelt, he cared about people's rights. He helped to pass fair laws for African Americans. He was one of many African Americans who worked to help people in his community, state, and nation. William Lloyd Garrison also fought for rights for African Americans. But unlike Richard Allen, he was from Massachusetts.

2. **Underline** how Richard Allen helped people.

PEARSON realize. Go online to access your interactive digital lesson.

157

What We Have in Common

Citizens in our communities, state, and country are similar. They want to help others. They act on their own beliefs. These citizens contribute in different ways.

Volunteers help people in our communities. They give food and clothing to people. They help people find shelter.

Leaders in our state are citizens. They work to help other citizens in our state. They make sure we have services like good schools and safe roads.

Citizens in our country help people, too. Today, our country's leaders want justice. They make sure laws are fair and equal for all people.

3. **Identify** individuals who show good citizenship. **Describe** ways they help others.

4. **Compare and Contrast** How were the lives and activities of Eleanor Roosevelt and Richard Allen alike? How were they different?

5. **What do many people in our communities, state, and country have in common?**

my Story Ideas

6. **Write** four sentences. Use a separate piece of paper. **Identify** how citizens help people in our community, state, and country. **Tell** about individualism, or how citizens can act on their own beliefs to help others. **Identify** three historical figures who have exhibited individualism and what they did to help others. **Tell** how citizens show good citizenship.

7. **Turn and talk** to a partner. **Tell** how Richard Allen showed inventiveness, or new ideas and ways of doing things.

PEARSON realize. Go online to access your interactive digital lesson.

159

Texas

Lesson 6

We Celebrate Our Nation

Envision It!

Circle things in the picture that show a celebration.

TEKS
1.A, 1.B, 2.A, 13.A

A **hero** is someone who works hard to help others. We remember national heroes on holidays. We remember special events on holidays, too.

Good citizens help people in our communities, state, and country. They can be heroes, too!

1. Why do we remember heroes?

_____

- - - - - - - - - - - - - - - - - -

_____

- - - - - - - - - - - - - - - - - -

UNLOCK
THE BIG
? I will know that we celebrate people and events from our nation's past.

Vocabulary

hero   president
nation

Our Nation's Heroes

Long ago, United States soldiers fought in a war. A holiday named Armistice Day was made to remember that war's end. People wanted to honor soldiers from other wars, too. So, the holiday was renamed Veterans Day in 1954. Veterans are men and women who fought for our country. We honor these brave people in November. People give speeches and we have parades on Veterans Day.

2. **Underline** the reason this holiday was changed to Veterans Day.

PEARSON
realize   Go online to access your interactive digital lesson.

161

George Washington

Abraham Lincoln

Heroes for Freedom

George Washington was a hero. Long ago, he was the leader of our country's army. He helped our nation become independent, or free. Washington became our first **president,** or leader of our country. We remember him on Presidents' Day in February.

Abraham Lincoln was a hero for freedom, too. He was president during a war in our country. At that time, many African Americans were not free. Lincoln helped make them free.

3. Circle the name of a hero you read about. **Underline** a contribution this hero made to our country.

Heroes for Justice

Martin Luther King Jr. is one of our heroes. We remember him on a holiday in January. King wanted all Americans to have the same, or equal, rights. He worked for justice. He made sure the laws of our nation were just, or fair for everyone. A **nation** is a group of people who have one government.

Martin Luther King Jr.

King asked our leaders to change unfair laws. He held them to their word. Laws were passed after Dr. King died. These laws gave African Americans equal rights.

4. **Write** about a contribution Martin Luther King Jr. made to our country.

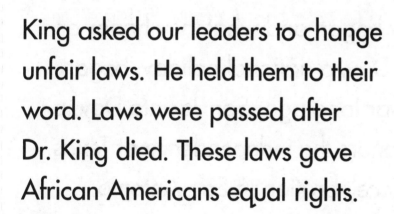

Holidays, Customs, and Celebrations

We celebrate and observe the origin of our nation, state, and community on holidays. Thanksgiving is one national holiday. Independence Day is another. On Independence Day, we remember how the United States gained its independence. It falls on July 4th every year.

You have read about customs, holidays, and celebrations, and about their origins. When you describe the origins of customs, holidays, and celebrations of communities, states, and nations, you talk about how they began and what they honor or celebrate. Veterans Day, a national holiday, began after the end of a war long ago. San Jacinto Day, a state celebration, honors the independence of Texas. Fiesta, a community celebration in San Antonio, honors the Alamo and the Battle of San Jacinto.

In the past, people celebrated Independence Day by ringing bells. They also marched in parades and gave speeches. Today, we march in parades and give speeches, too. We also have picnics and watch fireworks.

5.  **Compare and Contrast** <u>Underline</u> how people celebrate Independence Day differently today than they did in the past.

Got it?

TEKS 1.A, 1.B, 2.A, 13.A

6. ● **Main Idea and Details** What is the origin of Independence Day?

_____

_____

_____

7. ? How do you celebrate one of our national holidays?

 my Story Ideas

_____

_____

_____

8. **Write** a story about Dr. King. Use a separate piece of paper. **Tell** why he was a good citizen.

Folktales and Fables

The pictures show the story of Johnny Appleseed.

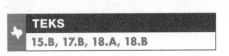

TEKS
15.B, 17.B, 18.A, 18.B

A community's literature, or written work, includes folktales, fables, and legends. A **folktale** is a story that is part of a group's culture. A **fable** is a story that teaches a lesson. It is a custom to tell these stories orally, or out loud. They pass on a community's beliefs, language, customs, and traditions.

Paul Bunyan

Folktales tell about make-believe characters like Paul Bunyan and his blue ox, Babe. Paul was big and strong. He cut down trees. His footprints made holes that filled with rain and became lakes!

1. Underline a storytelling custom.

Draw what you think Johnny will do next.

John Henry

Many folktales and fables use rich language. The story of John Henry is about a make-believe person. John Henry helped build the railroad. He used hammers to drill spikes into rocks. He did this faster than anyone else. He was strong, too. One day, railroad tracks had to go through a mountain. People thought a steam drill would be faster than John Henry. John Henry knew he was faster. *Pound, pound, pound* went John's hammers. He beat the steam drill!

2. ⊙ **Compare and Contrast**
   Underline ways John Henry was like Paul Bunyan.

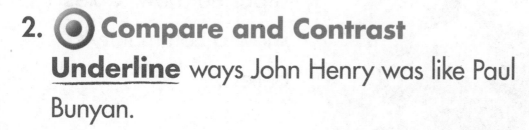

PEARSON realize | Go online to access your interactive digital lesson.

167

Aesop's Fables

Telling folktales, fables, and legends is a custom and tradition in many communities. Fables teach lessons about the community's beliefs.

The Ant and the Grasshopper is a fable about two friends. Ant was a hard worker. Grasshopper liked to play. Ant put away food for winter. But Grasshopper did not.

Ant had food to eat when winter came. His friend Grasshopper had no food. He was hungry. Grasshopper learned a lesson from Ant. It is important to work hard and be prepared!

3. **Underline** a community belief in the story. Explain to a partner how fables show a community's beliefs.

4.  **Compare and Contrast** How were Ant and Grasshopper different?

5. How are legends, folktales, and fables part of a community's culture?

 **my** Story Ideas

6. Turn and talk to a partner. **Tell** a story about an experience you had with your family.

7. Read literature, such as legends, folktales, and Aesop's fables. **Draw** a picture of your favorite story on a separate piece of paper. **Retell** the story to a partner. Use rich language to tell it.

Using Graphic Sources

Graphic sources are photographs, charts, or pictures. You can use them to get information. Look at the picture. Ask questions about what you see. Then try to find answers in the picture.

Look at this photograph. Where is this place? What kind of place is it? How do people there get from place to place? The photograph shows a city in China. Many people ride bicycles. Some people walk. Others drive cars.

Learning Objective

I will know how to use a graphic source.

TEKS

SS 6.C Identify and describe how the human characteristics of place such as activities are based upon geographic location.

SS 17.B Obtain information using visual sources such as pictures.

SS 18.B Interpret visual material.

ELA 14.D Use text features (e.g., illustrations) to locate information in text.

Look at the photograph below. **Write** what you see.

1. What kind of place is this?

_____

2. How do people get from place to place?

_____

PEARSON realize Go online to access your interactive digital lesson.

171

Lesson 1 TEKS 6.C

1. Draw something the people of a culture in a cold place might wear.

Lesson 2 TEKS 15.A

2. ◉ **Compare and Contrast Write** one way families are similar. **Write** one way families are different.

Similar:

_____

_____

Different: _____

_____

_____

 TEKS 15.A

3. Draw lines to match a culture word with a photograph.

tradition   music   language

Lesson 4 TEKS 1.A

4. On a separate piece of paper, describe the origins of customs, holidays, and celebrations of your community, state, and nation.

Lesson 5  TEKS 2.C, 13.A, 13.C

5. Look at the picture. **Fill in** the blank.

Good citizens _____

Lesson 6 TEKS 2.A

6. Write about a hero's contributions.

_____

_____

_____

Lesson 7 TEKS 15.B

7. Circle the best answer to finish the sentence.

The story about the Ant and the Grasshopper is

    A a fable.   **C** a true story.

    B a folktale.   **D** a song.

Go online to write and illustrate your own **myStory Book** using the **myStory Ideas** from this chapter.

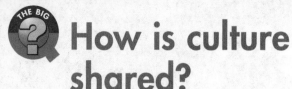 How is culture shared?

TEKS
SS 15.A, 18.B
ELA 17

In this chapter, you learned about people and cultures from many places.

Think about your own culture.

Draw a family custom. **Label** your drawing.

 PEARSON realize. Go online to access your interactive digital lesson.

175

Our Past, Our Present

my Story Spark

THE BIG ?

How does life change throughout history?

Draw a picture of what you would see if you could travel to the past.

my Story Video

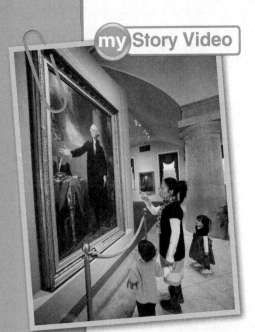

Texas Essential Knowledge and Skills

2.A Identify contributions of historical figures, including Sam Houston, George Washington, Abraham Lincoln, and Martin Luther King Jr., who have influenced the community, state, and nation.

2.B Identify historical figures such as Alexander Graham Bell, Thomas Edison, Garrett Morgan, and Richard Allen, and other individuals who have exhibited individualism and inventiveness.

2.C Compare the similarities and differences among the lives and activities of historical figures and other individuals who have influenced the community, state, and nation.

3.A Distinguish among past, present, and future.

3.B Describe and measure calendar time by days, weeks, months, and years.

3.C Create a calendar and simple timeline.

13.B Identify historical figures such as Benjamin Franklin, Francis Scott Key, and Eleanor Roosevelt who have exemplified good citizenship.

16.A Describe how technology changes the ways families live.

16.B Describe how technology changes communication, transportation, and recreation.

16.C Describe how technology changes the way people work.

17.A Obtain information about a topic using a variety of valid oral sources such as conversations, interviews, and music.

17.B Obtain information about a topic using a variety of valid visual sources such as pictures, symbols, electronic media, maps, literature, and artifacts.

17.C Sequence and categorize information.

18.B Create and interpret visual and written material.

 Begin With a Song

All Across the Country

Sing to the tune of "Skip to My Lou."

Long ago, we chopped down trees.

Built our houses, 1, 2, 3,

Life was simple all around me,

All across the country.

People in the kitchen, do, re, mi

Cakes on the table, 1, 2, 3

Sit on the benches, sit with me

All across the country.

PEARSON realize — Go online to access your interactive digital lesson.

177

Vocabulary Preview

clock

calendar

past

present

future

history

Identify examples of these words and (circle) them in the picture.

document

explorer

electricity

invention

communicate

transportation

Measuring Time

Put the letter *A* by the old dog.
Put the letter *B* by the young dog.

TEKS
3.B, 3.C, 17.C

We describe and **measure** calendar time in many ways. We talk about day and night. We also describe and measure time in days and weeks. There are 7 days in one week. The days of the week are Monday, Tuesday, Wednesday, Thursday, Friday, Saturday, and Sunday.

We describe and measure calendar time in months and years, too. There are 4 weeks in one month and 12 months in one year.

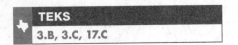

day

night

UNLOCK THE BIG ?

I will know that we use clocks and calendars to measure time.

Vocabulary

measure
clock
calendar

Clocks Measure Time

Clocks help us measure time. A **clock** shows seconds, minutes, and hours. We use clocks to know the time of day or night.

Some clocks have hands. One hand points to the hours. One hand points to the minutes. Some clocks also have a hand that shows seconds. Other clocks show the time using numbers.

1. **Underline** words on these two pages that are used to measure time.

PEARSON realize   Go online to access your interactive digital lesson.

181

Creating Calendars to Measure Time

A **calendar** shows the days, weeks, and months of the year. Each box on a calendar is one day.

You can create a calendar. First, write the month at the top of the page. Then, draw a chart with seven columns. Add rows to create a box for each day in the month. Write the days of the week in the first row. Write a date in each box. You can do this for each of the 12 months.

2. ◎ **Sequence** ⟨**Circle**⟩ the first day of the month on this calendar.

MAY

Sunday	Monday	Tuesday	Wednesday	Thursday	Friday	Saturday
1	2	3	4	5	6	7
8	9	10	11	12	13	14
15	16	17	18	19	20	21
22	23	24	25	26	27	28
29	30 Memorial Day	31				

3. ◎ **Compare and Contrast Write** how clocks and calendars are the same. **Write** how they are different.

_____

_____

_____

_____

4. ❓ How does a calendar help you measure time?

my Story Ideas

_____

_____

_____

_____

5. Create a calendar. Use a separate piece of paper. **Write** any special days of the month. Show family celebrations. Also show local, state, and national holidays. **Draw** symbols on the calendar to stand for special days. **Describe** how you measure time on your calendar. **Tell** a partner.

Sequence

Sequence is the order in which things happen. We use clue words to tell about order. Some clue words are *first*, *next*, and *last*.

Look at the pictures. Then read the sentences below. See how the sentences match the pictures.

Keisha was busy at school.

First, she read a book.

Next, she learned about magnets.

Last, she played a game.

| **First** | **Next** | **Last** |

Learning Objective

I will know how to put things in order.

TEKS

SS 17.C Sequence and categorize information.
ELA 14.C Retell the order of events in a text by referring to words and illustrations.

1. **Read** the paragraph below about what Carlos did on Saturday. **Underline** words that tell what happened first, next, and last.

> Carlos had fun on Saturday. First, he rode his bike. Next, he sorted his sports cards. Last, he played with his cat.

2. **Label** the pictures *first*, *next*, and *last*.

PEARSON realize Go online to access your interactive digital lesson.

185

Talking About Time

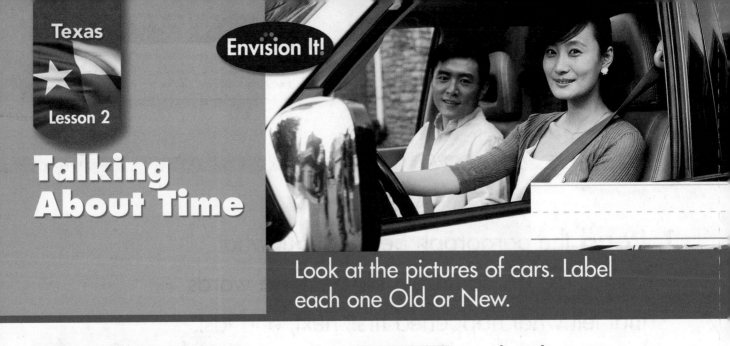

Look at the pictures of cars. Label each one Old or New.

TEKS
3.A, 17.B, 17.C

The **present** is what happens today. *Now* tells about the present.

The **past** is what happened before today. *Then* can tell about the past.

The **future** is what will happen after today. *Tomorrow* tells about the future.

People and places change over time. The girl in the picture has changed over time. In the past, she was 4 years old. She was shorter then. She is taller now.

1. **Underline** words that tell about time.

School Then and Now

Schools in the past were not like schools today. Children of all ages sat in the same classroom. Some children did not go to school.

Many more children go to school today. Children of the same age have their own classrooms. There are new tools like computers to help children learn today.

2. **◎ Compare and Contrast**
   (Circle) things in the picture that have changed from the past to the present.

Communities Then and Now

Communities change over time. Today, there are more cars, homes, and people. Buildings today are taller than in the past.

Look at these pictures. One picture shows a community in the past. The other picture shows the same community today.

3. **Circle** one thing in the pictures that has changed from the past to the present.

History tells the story of people and places from the past. History also tells about events that happened long ago. Some communities have parades that celebrate their history.

➡ TEKS 3.A

Got it?

4. 🎯 **Compare and Contrast** **Write** how you have changed over time.

Last year, I _____

Now, I _____

5. **?** Would you travel in time to the past or to the future? Why?

my Story Ideas

_____

_____

_____

6. Use a separate piece of paper. **Draw** three pictures of something from the past. Show it in the past, in the present, and what it may look like in the future.

Timelines

A timeline shows the order of events. You read a timeline from left to right. The earliest event is on the left. The latest event is on the right. The timeline below shows four events in Anila's life.

What happened in 2015? First, find that year on the timeline. Put your finger on that year. Then look at the picture and words below 2015. Anila learned to write in 2015.

A Timeline of Anila's Life

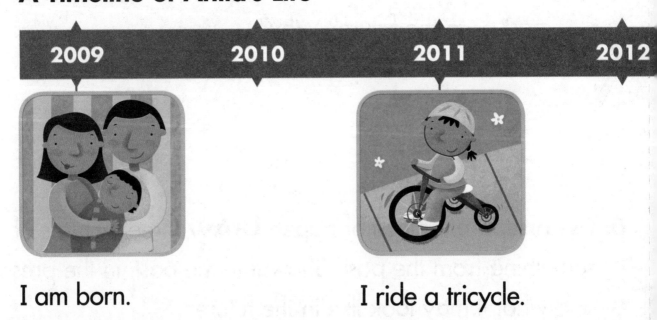

2009   2010   2011   2012

I am born.   I ride a tricycle.

TEKS

SS 3.C Create a simple timeline.
SS 17.C Sequence information.

Try it!

1. What could Anila do in 2011?

_____

2. **Circle** the earliest event shown on the timeline.

3. **Create** your own timeline like Anila's. Show important events.

| 2013 | 2014 | 2015 | 2016 |

My brother is born.　　　　　I learn to write.

PEARSON realize Go online to access your interactive digital lesson.

191

How We Learn About History

Photographs can show us about life in the past.

TEKS
17.A, 17.B, 17.C, 18.B

There are many ways to learn about history. You can interview people, or ask them questions. You can have a conversation, or talk, about the past.

You can learn from a **document**, or a paper with words on it. Photographs show how people and places looked. Songs tell how people felt. Artifacts, or objects made by people, show things used in the past.

1. ◉ **Main Idea and Details**
   Underline ways we get information about the past.

Draw what you learned about your past from an old photograph.

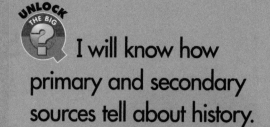
Vocabulary

document
primary source
secondary source

Primary Sources

We can categorize, or group, ways to learn about the past. Documents and photographs are primary sources. A **primary source** is written or made by a person who was at an event.

A map can be a primary source. It can show what a place looked like in the past. A letter can also be a primary source. We can read it to learn about the past.

2. Circle a primary source on this page.

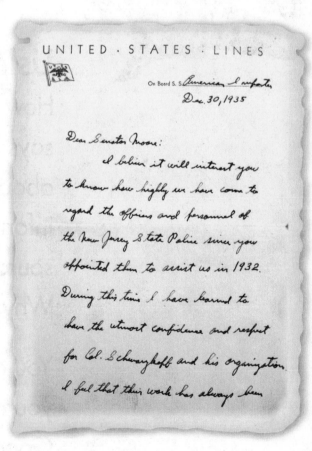

UNITED · STATES · LINES

On Board S. S. *American Importer*
Dec. 30, 1935

Dear Senator Moore:

I believe it will interest you to know how highly we have come to regard the officers and personnel of the New Jersey State Police since you appointed them to assist us in 1932. During this time I have learned to have the utmost confidence and respect for Col. Schwarzkopf and his organization. I feel that their work has always been

PEARSON **realize** Go online to access your interactive digital lesson.

193

Secondary Sources

A **secondary source** also tells about people, places, and events from the past. These sources were written or made after the event happened. Your schoolbooks and books in the library are secondary sources.

3. **Underline** a secondary source.

Using Sources

How can you know if what a source says is true? You can ask questions about the source. Where did the information come from? Who wrote the source? When was the source made? Why was the source made?

You can also read many sources. Then you can see if the facts are the same. Good sources give the same facts.

4. **Underline** two ways you can tell if what a source says is true.

5. ⊙ **Compare and Contrast Fill in** the chart to show how a photograph and a letter about a past event are different.

	Photograph	Letter
Same	primary source	primary source
Different		

6. You want to travel to a time in the past. How could you learn more about that time before you go?

my Story Ideas

7. **Find** an artifact. It can be an old toy, tool, or object from the past. **Think about** what it can tell you about people, places, and things. **Turn and talk** to a partner about it.

Texas

Lesson 4

American Heroes

Some coins show important people from the past.

TEKS
2.A, 2.C, 17.B, 18.B

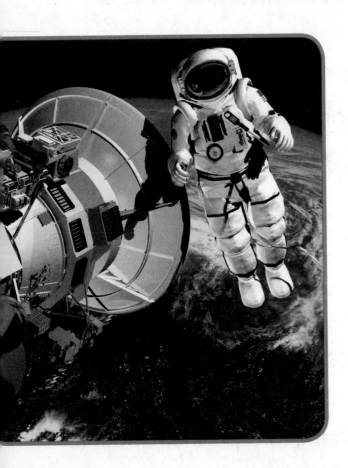

Heroes are people who work hard to help others. They are honest. People trust them. They face danger and must have courage. They take charge. They are responsible.

Heroes Explore

Some heroes are explorers. An **explorer** is a person who travels to learn about new places. Explorers go to places few people ever see. They go to new lands. They go under the ocean. They even go into space!

Draw your own coin that shows an important person.

UNLOCK THE BIG ? I will know about people who helped our country in the past.

Vocabulary
....
explorer

Long ago, people did not know how large our country was. Meriwether Lewis and William Clark went to find out. They were explorers. Lewis and Clark came back to tell others what they had seen.

They asked an American Indian woman, Sacagawea (sak uh juh WEE uh), to help them. They met other American Indians on their trip who did not speak English. Sacagawea helped them all talk to each other.

1. **Underline** the names of two explorers.

PEARSON realize Go online to access your interactive digital lesson.

197

Heroes Take Charge

Thomas Jefferson and Abraham Lincoln were both presidents of the United States. They were strong leaders and influenced their communities, states, and nation. Harriet Tubman and Abraham Lincoln also had something in common. They were similar in that they both helped African Americans to be free. But they had very different lives. Harriet Tubman was a poor African American who was not free. She went on to help more than 300 people to be free. Unlike Tubman, Abraham Lincoln was a free white man. And like Tubman, he helped African Americans to get their freedom when he was president.

You have also read about Martin Luther King Jr. on page 163. Like Harriet Tubman and Abraham Lincoln, he fought for the rights of African Americans. Unlike them, he lived in more recent times.

Thomas Jefferson

Harriet Tubman

2.  **Main Idea and Details** <u>Underline</u> a detail that tells about how Harriet Tubman helped others.

3. ◉ **Cause and Effect** Choose one of the people you read about. How did this hero change people's lives?

_____

_____

_____

4. **?** Which hero from the past would you
want to meet? Why?

_____

_____

_____

_____

5. **Draw** a Venn diagram. Use a separate piece of paper. **Write** the name of a hero over each circle. **List** details about their lives and activities. **Write** how their contributions were similar and how they were different.

PEARSON realize Go online to access your interactive digital lesson.

199

American Inventors

Circle things that help to make our lives easier.

TEKS
2.B, 2.C, 13.B, 17.B, 18.B

Benjamin Franklin

Inventors are people who think of something new, or a new way of doing things. They think for themselves and do not rely on others.

Benjamin Franklin

Benjamin Franklin believed people should think for themselves. He started one of the nation's first libraries. He started hospitals and fire departments, too. Franklin also invented a stove that warmed homes better than a fireplace.

1. **Circle** the main idea above.

UNLOCK THE BIG ? I will know why people invent useful things.

Vocabulary
....
inventor

Alexander Graham Bell

Alexander Graham Bell invented useful things like the telephone. He also helped people who could not hear learn how to speak.

Thomas Edison

Thomas Edison invented useful things, too. He made an electric light bulb to light homes. He made the phonograph, or record player. It recorded sounds.

2. ⊙ **Compare and Contrast Underline** ways Bell and Edison were similar.

Alexander Graham Bell

Thomas Edison

Garrett Morgan

Garrett Morgan

Garrett Morgan liked to invent useful things. He wanted to keep people safe, too.

Morgan was an independent thinker. He saw how firefighters put out fires. He saw how breathing in smoke made them sick.

Morgan invented a safety hood and smoke protector. He wore it to save people who were trapped in a tunnel. The hood kept him from breathing in dangerous gases. He sold his invention to fire departments in our country.

Morgan also made another safety invention. It was a traffic signal.

3. **Underline** why Garrett Morgan made inventions.

4. 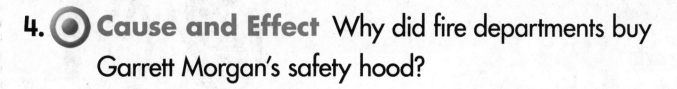 **Cause and Effect** Why did fire departments buy Garrett Morgan's safety hood?

_____

_____

_____

5.  How have inventions improved over time?

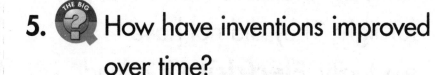my Story Ideas

_____

_____

_____

6. **Pick** an inventor and invention you read about. **Draw** a picture of the invention. Use a separate piece of paper. **Write** about the inventor. **Tell** why his invention is important.

7. **Turn and talk** to a partner. Tell how Benjamin Franklin showed good citizenship.

Life Then and Now

Envision It!

Which bike is from the past? Which bike is from the present?

TEKS
16.A, 16.B, 17.A, 17.B, 18.B

Long ago, families used oil lamps for light. They did not have electricity. **Electricity** is a kind of energy. Today, lamps use electricity.

Electricity was an important invention. An **invention** is something that is made for the very first time.

Inventions and technology change the way families live. Long ago, people washed clothes by hand. Today, we use a washing machine that runs on electricity. This invention makes life easier.

Write Past or Present by each bike.

UNLOCK THE BIG ? I will know how daily life has changed over time.

Vocabulary
electricity
invention

Daily Life Then and Now

People need food, clothing, and shelter. Long ago, many people grew their own food. People made their own clothing. They built homes for their families.

Today, we get the things we need in different ways. Most people buy food and clothing in stores. We live in homes other people build.

1. **⊙ Main Idea and Details**
   (Circle) the main idea in the second paragraph. **Underline** the details.

School, Work, and Play

Some children went to school long ago. Others learned at home. Most children did chores. They found wood for heat and cooking. They went out to get water. After chores, they played simple games. Technology has changed recreation. Today we play games on computers.

2. **Underline** how technology has changed recreation.

Families Then and Now

Every family has a history. You can look at photographs to learn about your family's past. You can interview family members about the past. Ask about school, work, and play.

3. **Write** one way you can learn about your family history.

4. ◎ **Compare and Contrast Complete** the chart.
Write how life has changed from the past to the
present.

Past	Present
oil lamp	_electricity_
made clothing	
grew food	

5. **What one thing do you think has**
changed the most from the past to the present?

my Story Ideas

6. **Draw** two pictures. Use separate pieces of paper. First,
draw a picture of how technology has changed the way
your family lives. Next, draw a picture of how technology
has changed recreation, or activities you do. **Describe**
each picture to a partner.

Technology Then and Now

Envision It!

Circle ways you stay in touch with friends.

TEKS
16.B, 16.C, 17.B, 18.B

How can you talk to friends who live far away? You can call them. You can ride on a bus to visit them. Long ago, you could not do these things.

Communication Then

We **communicate** when we share information with others. Long ago, people had no telephones. They sent each other letters. This was a slow way to communicate. The letters were delivered on horseback. It took weeks to get a letter!

UNLOCK
THE BIG
?

I will know how communication and transportation have changed over time.

Vocabulary

communicate
e-mail   transportation

Communication Now

Technology changes the way we communicate. Airplanes carry letters around the world. Now, it takes only a few days to get a letter.

We can use computers to communicate. An **e-mail** is a message sent through a computer. It takes seconds to get an e-mail!

Technology changes the way we work, too. We use computers to connect to the Internet. It helps us work and communicate.

1. **Underline** words that tell about technology we use.

PEARSON
realize   Go online to access your
interactive digital lesson.

209

Transportation Then

Transportation is the way we move from place to place. Long ago, there were no cars or trains. People rode horses or walked to get from place to place. Some people rode in wagons pulled by horses. They traveled over water in small ships. It took months to travel a long way.

Transportation Now

Transportation is much faster today. We use cars, buses, and trains. We travel over water in large ships. We can fly in airplanes to visit places far away. Cars, trains, and airplanes are fast. Today, we can travel a long way in a day.

2. ◎ **Main Idea and Details**
   (Circle) the main idea in the paragraph above. **Underline** two details.

3. ◎ **Compare and Contrast Describe** to a partner two ways people traveled in the past. **Describe** two ways we travel today.

4. What is one way that technology has changed the way we communicate?

my Story Ideas

_____

- - - - - - - - - - - - - - - - - - -

_____

_____

5. Draw a chart. Use a separate piece of paper. **Write** Transportation and Communication at the top. **Draw** pictures that show examples of each word. **Turn** to a partner. **Describe** how technology has changed the way people live and work.

6. Turn and talk to a partner. **Tell** how we obtain information from electronic media such as computers and televisions.

PEARSON
realize. Go online to access your interactive digital lesson.

211

Lesson 1  TEKS 3.B, 3.C

1. What words can we use to describe and measure time on a calendar?

Lesson 2 TEKS 3.A, 17.C

2. Circle words that tell about time.

then	tomorrow	school
today	home	past
friends	now	present
long ago	future	clothing

3.  **Sequence** **Write** the word that comes next.

past, present, _____

4. Draw a line from each word to the correct picture.

photograph

document

5. How were the contributions of Abraham Lincoln and Harriet Tubman similar?

_____

_____

Lesson 5  TEKS 2.B, 13.B

6. How were the inventors you read about similar?

Lesson 6 TEKS 16.A

7. Complete the sentence. **Write** one way life in the past without technology was different than life today.

Long ago,

Lesson 7 TEKS 16.B

8. Read the question and circle the best answer.
Which kind of transportation uses the newest technology?

A horse

C airplane

B wagon

D bicycle

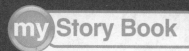

Go online to write and illustrate your own **myStory Book** using the **myStory Ideas** from this chapter.

How does life change throughout history?

TEKS
SS 3.A, 18.B
ELA 17

Think about your travel back in time.

Draw something you "saw" in the past.

Atlas

The United States of America, Political

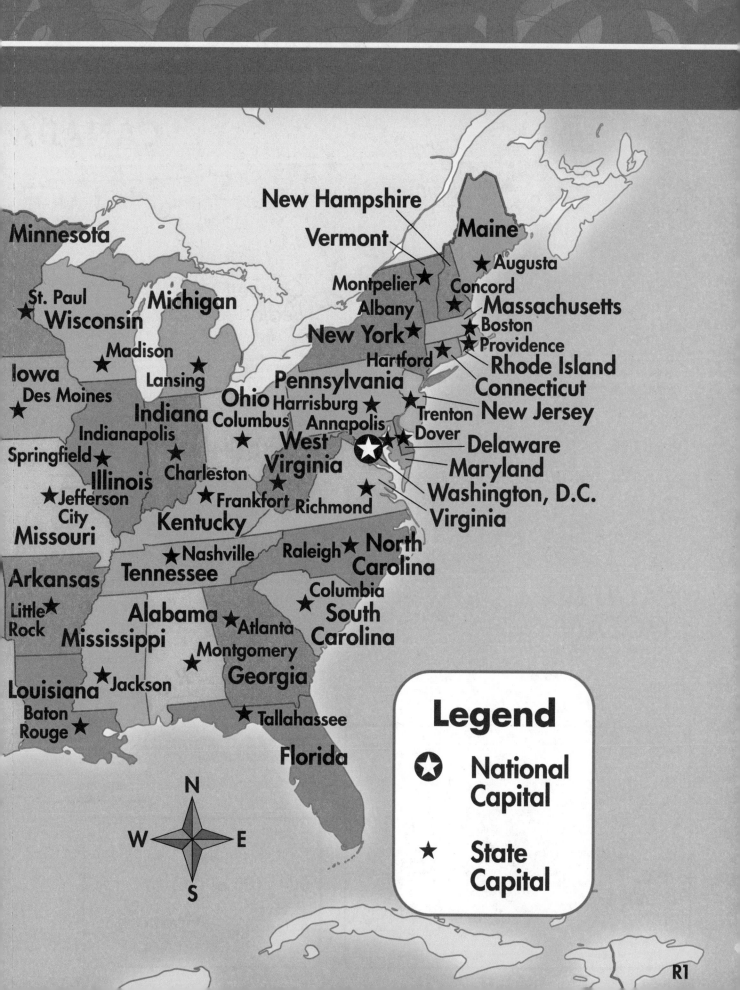

Minnesota

St. Paul
Wisconsin

Madison

Iowa
Des Moines

Michigan

Lansing

Indiana

Indianapolis

Springfield

Illinois

Jefferson
City

Missouri

Charleston

Frankfort

Kentucky

Arkansas

Little
Rock

Nashville

Tennessee

Alabama

Mississippi

Montgomery

Jackson

Georgia

Louisiana

Baton
Rouge

Tallahassee

Florida

New Hampshire

Vermont

Maine

Augusta

Montpelier

Concord

Albany

Massachusetts

Boston

New York

Providence

Hartford

Rhode Island

Pennsylvania

Connecticut

Ohio

Harrisburg

Trenton

New Jersey

Columbus

Annapolis

Dover

West
Virginia

Delaware

Maryland

Washington, D.C.

Richmond

Virginia

Raleigh

North
Carolina

Columbia

South
Carolina

Atlanta

N

W   E

S

Legend

⭐ National
Capital

★ State
Capital

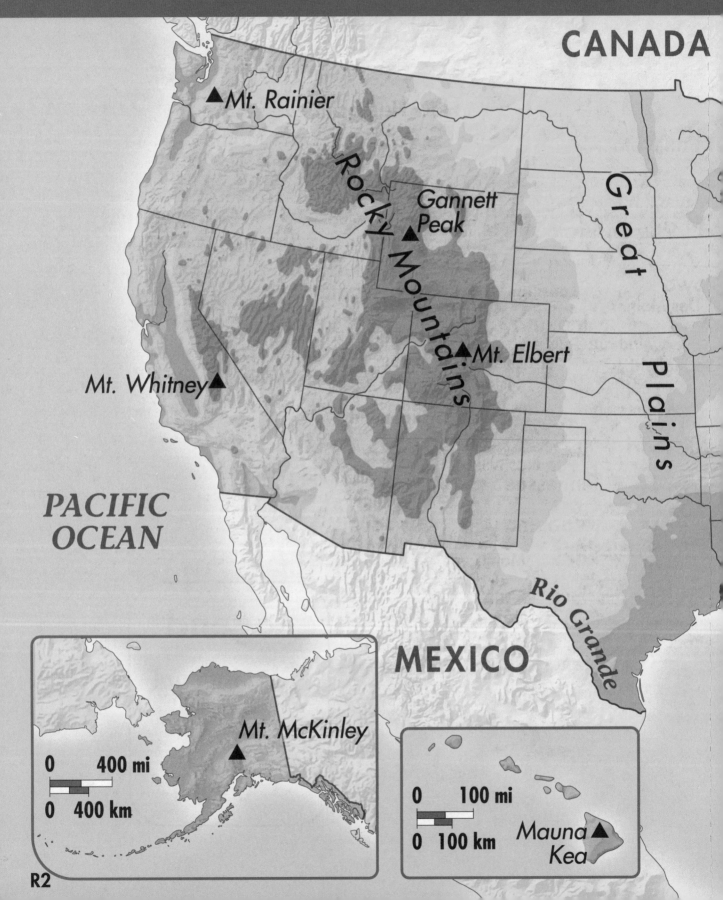

CANADA

▲ Mt. Rainier

Rocky Mountains

Gannett
Peak ▲

Great

Plains

▲ Mt. Elbert

Mt. Whitney ▲

PACIFIC
OCEAN

Rio Grande

MEXICO

Mt. McKinley ▲

0   400 mi

0   400 km

0   100 mi

0   100 km

Mauna
Kea ▲

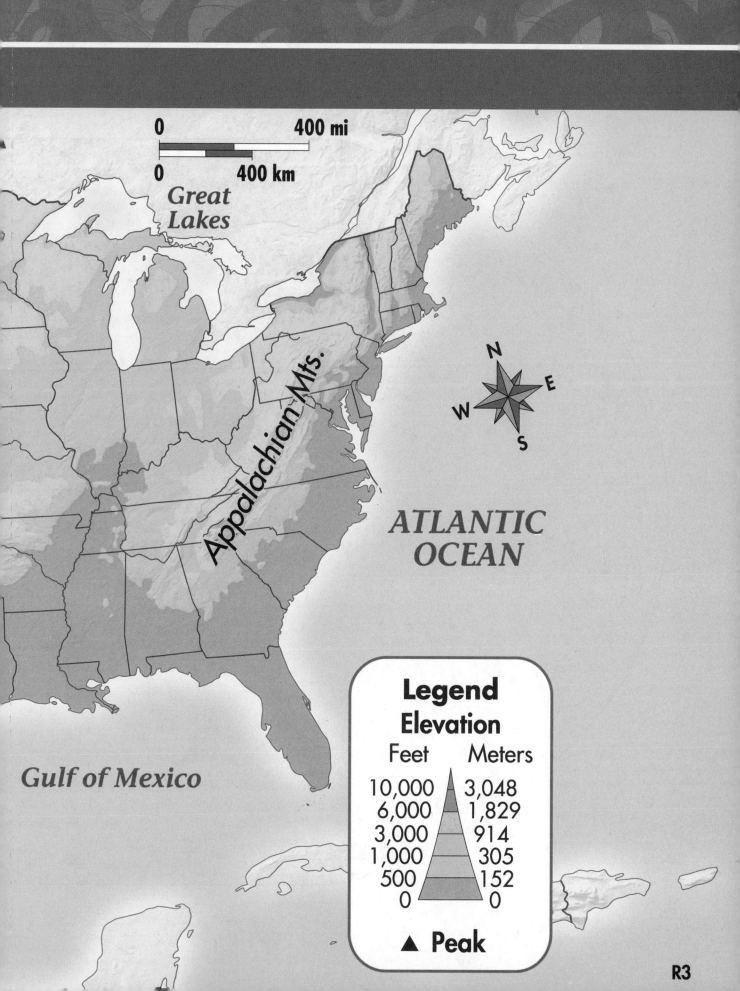

0   400 mi

0   400 km

Great Lakes

Appalachian Mts.

ATLANTIC OCEAN

N
W   E
S

Gulf of Mexico

Legend
Elevation

Feet	Meters
10,000	3,048
6,000	1,829
3,000	914
1,000	305
500	152
0	0

▲ Peak

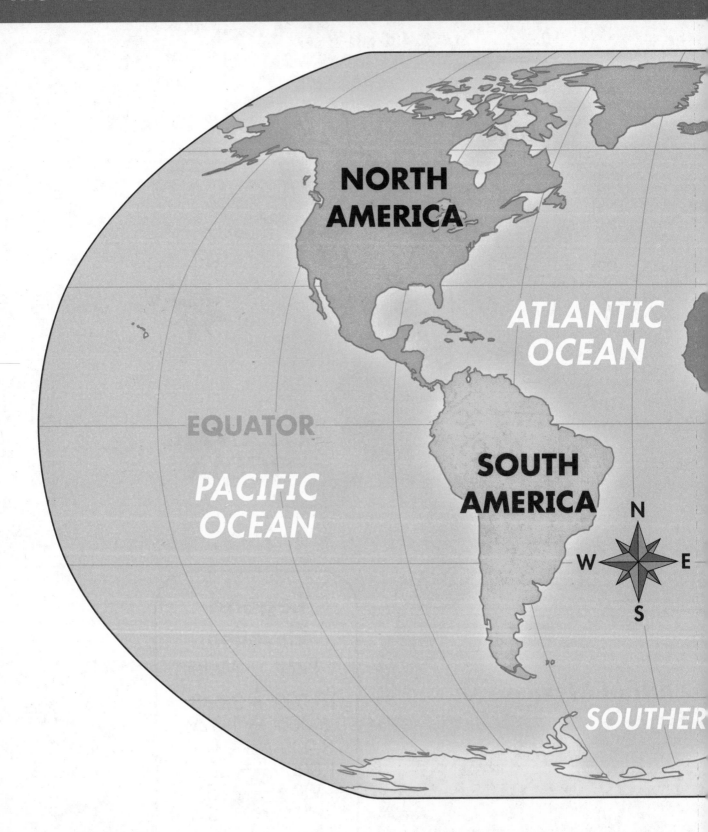

NORTH
AMERICA

ATLANTIC
OCEAN

EQUATOR

PACIFIC
OCEAN

SOUTH
AMERICA

N

W   E

S

SOUTHER

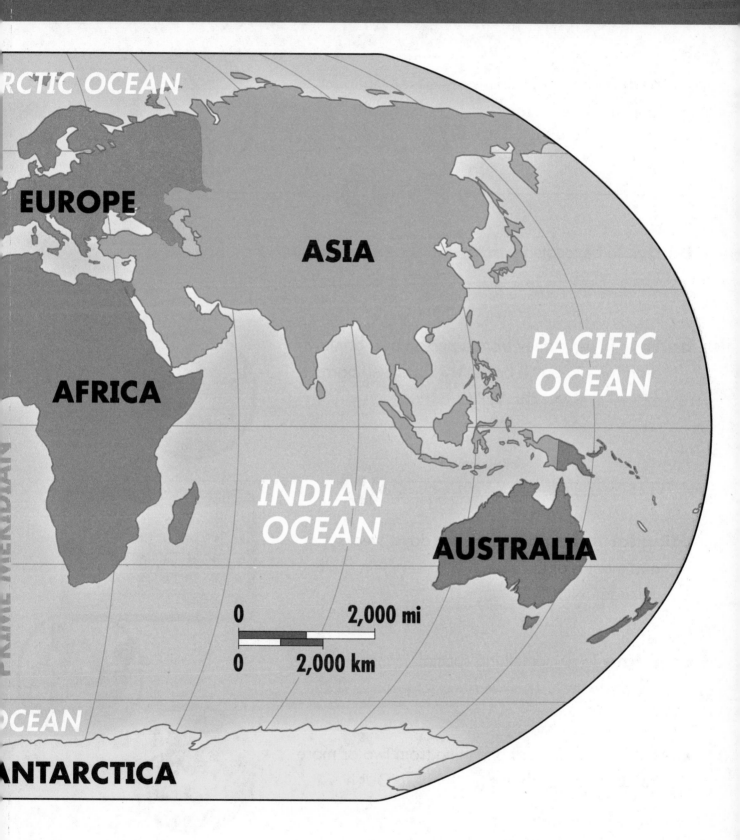

ARCTIC OCEAN

EUROPE

ASIA

AFRICA

PACIFIC
OCEAN

INDIAN
OCEAN

AUSTRALIA

PRIME MERIDIAN

OCEAN

ANTARCTICA

0   2,000 mi

0   2,000 km

Glossary

A

anthem A song of praise. We sing our national anthem every morning at school. NOUN

B

border To be located next to. Four states border Texas. VERB

borrow To get money from a person or a bank with a promise to pay it back. My father will borrow money to buy a car. VERB

C

calendar A chart that shows the days, weeks, and months of the year. May is a month on the calendar. NOUN

celebrate To do something special. We will celebrate my sister's wedding tomorrow. VERB

choice The selection of one thing from two or more things. I have a choice of games. NOUN

citizen A member of a state or country. I am a citizen of the United States. NOUN

clock A tool that shows what time it is. There is a big clock in our classroom. NOUN

colony An area that is ruled by another country. Florida was once a colony of Spain. NOUN

communicate To share information with other people. People communicate by phone. VERB

community The place where people live, work, and play. My community has a parade on Memorial Day. NOUN

consumer Someone who buys or uses goods and services. My father is a consumer when he buys food. NOUN

continent A very large piece of land. North America is a continent. NOUN

contribute To give in order to help a group. I will contribute my time to help out at the food drive. VERB

Plymouth Colony

ATLANTIC OCEAN

Poor soil

Original Mayflower landing site

Plymouth

Cape Cod

Better farmland

NORTH AMERICA

ATLANTIC OCEAN

PACIFIC OCEAN

SOUTH AMERICA

cooperate To work together. We **cooperate** to keep the classroom neat. VERB

culture The way a group of people lives. Celebrating holidays is a part of **culture**. NOUN

custom The way people usually do something. It is a **custom** for people to shake hands when they meet. NOUN

D

desert A very dry area. A **desert** gets little rain. NOUN

direction A word that tells which way to go or where something is. East is one **direction** on a map. NOUN

document A paper with words on it. The Constitution is an important **document**. NOUN

E

electricity A kind of energy. Our oven uses electricity. NOUN

e-mail Electronic mail or a message sent through a computer. I sent him an **e-mail**. NOUN

explorer A person who travels to unknown places to find out what is there. An astronaut is an explorer. NOUN

F

fable A story that is made up to teach a lesson. I learned a lesson when I read the **fable** "The Ant and the Grasshopper." NOUN

family A group of people who live together. I have a large **family**. NOUN

fiesta A public celebration with dancing and music. We will hear music at the **fiesta**. NOUN

folktale A story that is part of a community's culture. The **folktale** about Paul Bunyan is make-believe. NOUN

freedom A person's right to make choices. People have the **freedom** to vote in our country. NOUN

future What will happen after today. I want to be an astronaut in the **future**. NOUN

G

globe A round model of Earth. I can find North America on a **globe**. NOUN

goods Things that workers make or grow. You can buy **goods** such as fruit at the market. NOUN

government A group of citizens who work together to make rules and laws. Our state **government** passed a recycling law. NOUN

governor The leader of a state. Our **governor** wants us to help keep our parks clean. NOUN

H

hero Someone who works hard to help others. A firefighter is a **hero** who helps save lives. NOUN

hill A raised area of land, like a mountain but not as high. I live on top of a **hill**. NOUN

history The story of people, places, and events from the past. I study **history** in school. NOUN

holiday A special day. Kwanzaa is a **holiday** that my family celebrates. NOUN

I

independence Freedom. Texas won its **independence** from Mexico. NOUN

invention Something that is made for the very first time. The washing machine is a useful **invention**. NOUN

inventors People who think of something new. Benjamin Franklin is one of the **inventors** I read about. NOUN

J

job The work people do. My **job** at home is to wash the dishes. NOUN

L

lake A large body of water with land around it. We rowed a boat on the **lake**. NOUN

language The words we speak. My family speaks more than one **language**. NOUN

law A rule that everyone must obey. Our state has a **law** about wearing seatbelts. NOUN.

leader Someone who helps people decide what to do. The coach is a **leader** in my school. NOUN

legend A list of what symbols on a map mean. I used the **legend** to find the park. NOUN

M

map A drawing of a place that shows where things are. We used a **map** to find the way to your house. NOUN

market A place where goods are sold. My mother buys bread at the **market**. NOUN

mayor The main leader in a town or city. Ms. Garcia is the **mayor** of my town. NOUN

measure To divide something into parts that can be counted. We **measure** time in hours and days. VERB

mission A center where Spanish priests lived and worked. The Alamo began as a Catholic **mission**. NOUN

money Coins or bills that people use to buy things. The game cost a lot of **money**. NOUN

mountain The highest kind of land. There is snow at the top of the **mountain**. NOUN

N

nation A group of people who have one government. The president is the leader of our nation. NOUN

needs Things that people must have to live. Food and clothing are **needs**. NOUN

O

ocean A large body of salt water. We swim in the ocean every summer. NOUN

P

past What has happened before today. I learned to ride a bike in the **past**. NOUN

phonograph An invention that plays records. The phonograph was invented by Thomas Edison. NOUN

pledge A promise to be loyal. I say a **pledge** to the flag. NOUN

present The time that is happening now. Schools are different in the **present** than they were in the past. NOUN

president The leader of our country. People vote to choose the **president**. NOUN

primary source Something written or made by a person who was at an event. A photograph is one kind of **primary source**. NOUN

producer Someone who makes or grows goods. A farmer is a **producer**. NOUN

R

recycle To make something new from something that has been used before. When we **recycle** paper, it can be made into new paper. VERB

reduce To use less of something. We can **reduce** the amount of water we use. VERB

responsibility Something a person should do. Feeding our dog is my **responsibility**. NOUN

right Something that people are free to do or have. You have a **right** to attend school. NOUN

river A long body of water that often moves over land toward a lake or an ocean. We sailed our boat down the **river**. NOUN

S

save To put money away to use at another time. I will **save** my money to buy the book. VERB

scarce Not enough of something. Most plants do not grow if water is **scarce**. ADJECTIVE

secondary source Something written or made by a person after an event happened. A history book is a **secondary source**. NOUN

services Work that people do for others. Teaching and coaching are **services**. NOUN

shelter A place to live. Everyone needs food, clothing, and **shelter**. NOUN

symbol Something that stands for something else. Our country's flag is a **symbol** of the United States. NOUN

T

trade To give something in return for something else. My friend and I like to **trade** books. VERB

tradition A way to do something that people pass down over time. It is a **tradition** in my family to eat a meal together on Sunday. NOUN

transportation The way people move from place to place. We use buses for **transportation**. NOUN

V

vote To make a choice that is counted. One day I will be able to **vote** for the president. VERB

W

wants Things we would like to have. Some of my **wants** are a game and skates. NOUN

weather What it is like outside at a certain place and time. I hope the **weather** is good for our picnic. NOUN

Index

This index lists the pages on which topics appear in this book. Page numbers followed by *m* refer to maps. Page numbers followed by *p* refer to photographs. Page numbers followed by *c* refer to charts or graphs. Page numbers followed by *t* refer to timelines. Bold page numbers indicate vocabulary definitions. The terms *See* and *See also* direct the reader to alternate entries.

Credits

Text Acknowledgments

Grateful acknowledgement is made to the following for copyrighted material:

Page 9

Song "Texas, Our Texas," music by William J. Marsh, lyrics by Gladys Yoakum Wright & William J. Marsh.

Maps

XNR Productions, Inc.

Photographs

Photo locators denoted as follows: Top (T), Center (C), Bottom (B), Left (L), Right (R), Background (Bkgd)

Cover

Front Cover (TL) Soccer game, Robin Russell/Alamy; (TR) Astronaut and spacecraft, 1971yes/Shutterstock; (CC) Girl on bus, Bikeriderlondon/Shutterstock; (CR) State capitol, Austin, Pearson Education; (BC) Eagle, visuelldesign/Shutterstock.
Back Cover (TR) Texas flag, soleilc1/Fotolia; (CC) Armadillo, SunnyS/Fotolia; (CR) Man and boy, Pearson Education; (BC) Rodeo, JustStockPhotos/Alamy.

Text

Front Matter

x: Comstock Images/AGE Fotostock; xi: Martin Wierink/Alamy; xii: Pearson Education; xiii: Pearson Education; xiv: Rhea Anna/Getty

Celebrate Texas and the Nation

001: Bill Bachmann/Alamy; 002: ZUMA Press, Inc./Alamy; 005: Rob Wilson/Shutterstock; 007: Pearson Education; 008: michaeljung/Fotolia; 010: Comstock/AGE Fotostock; 011: Smiley N. Pool, Houston Chronicle/AP Images; Ronnie Wilson/Alamy

Chapter 01

012: Pearson Education; 016: Ariel Skelley/Blend Images/Getty Images; 017: Comstock Images/AGE Fotostock; 020: Dorling Kindersley Media Library; 021: Tyler Olson/Fotolia; 022: Pearson Education; 023: Frank Siteman/PhotoEdit; 026: fc1/picturesbyrob/Alamy; 027: Designpics/Glow Images; 027: Pearson Education; 028: Karen Kasmauski/Terra/Corbis; 028: Tetra Images/Getty Images; 029: Spencer Grant/Science Source; 029: wong sze yuen/Shutterstock; 030: Pearson Education; 032: Lacy Atkins/Corbis News/Corbis; 034: iStockphoto/Thinkstock; 035: Dennis MacDonald/PhotoEdit; 036: Education & Exploration 2/Alamy Stock Photo; 037: Stewart Cohen/Blend Images/Getty Images; 038: Elena Yakusheva/Shutterstock; 039: Christopher Halloran/Shutterstock; 039: David R. Frazier

Photolibrary, Inc./Alamy; 040: ZUMA Press, Inc./Alamy; 042: henri conodul/PhotoLibrary; 043: Thomas Del Brase/Photographer's Choice RF/Getty Images; 044: David Madison/Getty Images; 044: Jupiterimages/liquidlibrary/Thinkstock; 044: Lagui/Shutterstock; 045: Dorling Kindersley; 045: James Steidl/Fotolia; 045: Jupiterimages/Photos.com/thinkstock; 046: Stock Montage/SuperStock; 047: Comstock/Thinkstock; 048: lawcain/Fotolia; 048: Rich Koele/Shutterstock; Jules Selmes/Pearson Education Ltd; stephen jones/Fotolia; ZUMA Press, Inc./Alamy

Chapter 02

054: Pearson Education; 059: IE127/Image Source/Alamy; 060: Maria Spann/Getty Images; 060: Ray Kachatorian/Getty Images; 062: charlie bonallack/Alamy; 062: Creatas Images/Thinkstock; 062: Pixtal/SuperStock; 063: Masterfile; 063: Peter Beck/Corbis; 063: WoodyStock/Alamy; 064: Dave Nagel/Getty Images; 068: Bon Appetit/Alamy; 068: Danny E Hooks/Shutterstock; 068: Kai Wong/Shutterstock; 069: Eye Ubiquitous/SuperStock; 069: verdateo/Fotolia; 069: WavebreakmediaMicro/Fotolia; 070: blue jean images/Getty Images; 070: Christopher Futcher/E+/Getty Images; 074: Hemera Technologies/Thinkstock; 075: Pearson Education; 076: Monkey Business/Fotolia; 078: Exactostock/SuperStock; 078: SuperStock; 079: Image Source/Getty Images; 079: Pedro Nogueira/Shutterstock; 079: Photos.com/Thinkstock; 083: Kevin Dodge/Corbis; 084: Andersen Ross/Blend Images/Getty Images; 084: Shalom Ormsby/Blend Images/Corbis; 085: Islandstock/Alamy; 085: Kadmy/Fotolia; 086: H. Edward Kim/National Geographic/Getty Images; 086: Kathryn Scott Osler/Denver Post/Getty Images; 088: Martin Wierink/Alamy; 088: Pedro Nogueira/Shutterstock; 089: Islandstock/Alamy; 089: Pearson Education; 089: Pixtal/SuperStock

Chapter 03

092: Pearson Education; 102: Gorilla/Fotolia; 102: JGI/Jamie Grill/Blend Images/Getty Images; 103: Serg64/Shutterstock; 108: AdamEdwards/Shutterstock; 109: Jupiterimages/Thinkstock; 109: Phil Emmerson/Shutterstock; 109: Wendy Connett/Robert Harding World Imagery/Getty Images; 110: Dorling Kindersley Media Library; 110: Medioimages/Photodisc/Thinkstock; 110: Milosz Aniol/Shutterstock; 112: NPA/Stone/Getty Images; 113: Pearson Education; 116: Ariel Skelley/Blend Images/Corbis; 116: iStockphoto/Thinkstock; 118: Jim West/Alamy; 119: iStockphoto/Thinkstock; 120: Pavel Losevsky/Fotolia; 120: Sripfoto/Fotolia; 120: Steve Smith/Purestock/SuperStock; 122: altrendo travel/Getty Images; 123: Vasca/Shutterstock; 124: Maksim Toome/Shutterstock; 124: Ocean/Corbis; 124: Ssguy/Shutterstock; 125: EuroStyle Graphics/Alamy; 125: iStockphoto/Thinkstock; 126: Erin Patrice O'Brien/Photodisc/Getty Images; 126: moodboard/Corbis; 126: Stockbyte/Thinkstock; 173: Steve Peixotto/Getty Images; John Foxx Collection. Imagestate; MIXA Co., Ltd

Chapter 04

157: Monkey Business/Fotolia; 132: Pearson Education; 136: cantor pannatto/Fotolia; 136: Newscom; 136: Valerie Kuypers/AFP/Getty Images; 136: XiXinXing/Getty Images; 137: Cindy Hopkins/Alamy; 137: Jerod Foster/Icon SMI CDM/Newscom; 138: Bon Appetit/Alamy; 138: Danny E Hooks/Shutterstock; 138: Kai Wong/Shutterstock; 138: Pearson Education; 139: Masterfile Corporation; 140: David P. Smith/Shutterstock; 140: Gary Yim/Shutterstock; 142: Creatas Images/Thinkstock; 142: JGI/Tom Grill/Blend Images/Corbis; 142: Sonya etchison/Shutterstock; 143: Ronnie Kaufman/Corbis; 144: Atlantide Phototravel/Corbis; 146: Keren Su/Corbis; 146: Seiya Kawamoto/Thinkstock; 147: Steve Peixotto/Getty Images; 148: Cultura/Alamy; 148: Hugh Sitton/Corbis; 150: Masterfile Corporation; 151: Pearson Education; 152: David J. Phillip/AP Images; 154: Medioimages/Photodisc/Thinkstock; 154: Tatjana Strelkova/Shutterstock; 155: Pearson Education; 156: Alexander Raths/Fotolia; 156: Everett Collection/Newscom; 156: Vvvita/Fotolia; 157: bikeriderlondon/Shutterstock; 157: Niday Picture Library/Alamy; 158: Brand X Pictures/Stockbyte/Getty Images; 160: Bob Daemmrich/Alamy; 161: Ocean/Corbis; 162: Library of Congress Prints and Photographs Division[LC-DIG-pga-01368]; 162: Library of Congress Prints and Photographs Division[LC-USZ62-4063]; 163: Bob Adelman/Magnum Photos; 164: Comstock/Thinkstock Images; 170: Nataliya Hora/Shutterstock; 171: iStockphoto/Thinkstock; 173: JGI/Tom Grill/Blend Images/Corbis; 173: Keren Su/CORBIS; 173: Masterfile; 173: Monkey Business/Fotolia; 174: Michael H/Digital Vision/Getty Images

Chapter 05

176: Greg Dale/National Geographic Society/Corbis; 180: Kevin R. Morris/Bohemian Nomad Picturemakers/Corbis; 180: Pearson Education; 181: Edwin Remsberg/Alamy; 184: Pearson Education; 184: Pearson Education; 185: Pearson Education; 186: View Stock/Alamy; 187: Ariel Skelley/Corbis; 187: Everett Collection/Superstock; 187: Library of Congress Prints and Photographs Division[LC-DIG-ppmsc-04830]; 188: Underwood & Underwood/Corbis; 189: Gary Conner/PhotoEdit; 192: Darren Modricker/Corbis; 192: Rhea Anna/Photolibrary/Getty Images; 193: Bettmann/Corbis; 194: Gelpi/Shutterstock; 196: 1971yes/Shutterstock; 196: Atlaspix/Shutterstock; 196: NewsCom; 196: United States Mint; 197: Washington State Historical Society/Art Resource, NY; 198: AP Images; 198: World History Archive/Alamy; 200: B Christopher/Alamy; 200: Library of Congress Prints and Photographs Division Washington, D.C.[HABS SC,43-STATBU,1–28]; 200: Scanrail/Fotolia; 201: Education Images/Universal Images Group Limited/Alamy; 201: Stapleton Historical Collection/Heritage Image Partnership Ltd/Alamy; 201: Steve Gorton/Dorling Kindersley; 202: Fotosearch/Archive Photos/Getty Images; 204: imagebroker.net/SuperStock; 204: Kate Kunz/Corbis; 205: Edouard Debat-Ponsan/The Bridgeman Art Library/Getty Images; 205: Monkey Business Images/Shutterstock; 205: sequarell/Shutterstock; 206: Ocean/Corbis; 211: ZouZou/Shutterstock; 212: Nancy Carter/North Wind Picture Archives/Alamy; 213: Bettmann/Corbis; 213: Underwood & Underwood/Corbis

Glossary

R08: Jamie Grill/Getty Images; R08: Monkey Business/Fotolia; R08: Pearson Education; R08: Shalom Ormsby/Blend Images/Corbis; R09: Brand X Pictures/Stockbyte, Getty Images, Inc.; R09: Comstock Images/AGE Fotostock; R09: Stockbyte/Thinkstock; R10: Bettmann/CORBIS; R10: Newscom; R10: Pearson Education; R10: Ronnie Kaufman/Corbis; R10: Wendy Connett/Robert Harding World Imagery/Getty Images; R11: Creatas/Thinkstock; R11: Greg Sorber/Albuquerque Journal/ZUMA Press, Inc./Alamy; R11: NASA; R11: Steve Peixotto/Getty Images; R11: ZouZo/Shutterstock; R12: 1971yes/Shutterstock; R12: B Christopher/Alamy; R12: henri conodul/PhotoLibrary; R12: Hermera/Thinkstock; R12: Serg64/Shutterstock; R12: Thinkstock; R13: Thinkstock Images; R13: AP Images/David J. Phillip; R13: Dennis MacDonald/PhotoEdit; R13: Gary Conner/PhotoEdit; R13: Kate Kunz/Corbis; R14: iStockphoto/Thinkstock; R14: Lawrence Migdale/Getty Images; R14: Milosz Aniol/Shutterstock; R14: Pearson Education; R14: Ron Buskirk/Alamy; R15: Image Source/Getty Images; R15: Phil Emmerson/Shutterstock; R15: Rob Wilson/Shutterstock; R16: Ariel Skelley/Corbis; R16: Christopher Halloran/Shutterstock; R16: Comstock Images/AGE Fotostock; R16: Education Images/Universal Images Group Limited/Alamy; R16: Heritage Image Partnership Ltd/Alamy; R16: Library of Congress Prints and Photographs Division [LC-DIG-ppmsc-04830]; R16: Medioimages/Photodisc/Thinkstock; R16: Mike Flippo/Shutterstock; R16: Rhea Anna/Photolibrary/Getty Images; R16: Wally McNamee/Corbis; R17: Ariel Skelley/Blend Images/Corbis; R17: Dorling Kindersley Media Library; R17: Dorling Kindersley Media Library/DK IMAGES; R17: Exactostock/SuperStock; R17: Superstock; R17: Tyler Olson/Fotolia; R18: Comstock Image/Jupiter Images/Thinkstock; R18: David P. Smith/Shutterstock; R18: Jupiterimages/Photos.com/thinkstock; R18: Masterfile; R18: Pearson Education; R19: EuroStyle Graphics/Alamy; R19: IE127/Image Source/Alamy; R19: Pearson Education; R19: Steve Smith/Purestock/SuperStock; Ronnie Wilson/Alamy; Sabena Jane Blackbird/Alamy